AN AMERICAN DESTROYER

USS *Hamner* (DD-718)

KENNETH ERICKSEN

Edited by: Patty Hathaway

PAGE PUBLISHING
Conneaut Lake, PA

First originally published by Page Publishing 2022

ISBN 979-8-88793-485-3 (pbk)
ISBN 979-8-88793-471-6 (digital)

Printed in the United States of America

CONTENTS

FOREWORD

I consider myself fortunate to have known the late Ken Ericksen. My husband remembers Ken vividly as the first shipmate to approach him at the first reunion we attended in 2006, handing Merrill a set of the *Hamner* history cards he had created. It became obvious to us that the *Hamner* Association had a valuable asset in their historian. For over ten years since then, I had the privilege of working with Ken when I needed information on the history of the *Hamner* or the association. Photographing him during reunions and capturing that wonderful smile for the annual reunion book was always a pleasure.

Why was I willing to become the editor for Ken's book? There are many reasons. First and foremost is my love and appreciation for our veterans. I have spent many years supporting veterans, such as volunteering for the American Legion in my hometown before I was eligible for membership, and then joining the AL Auxiliary when I became eligible. I have attended fifteen *Hamner* reunions since 2006, and since 2009, I have served as an officer of the association. As an officer, one of my primary responsibilities is to receive, record, and preserve all of the historical documents, photographs, and other memorabilia from shipmates and their families. Because of this role, when Ken started this book, I was one of the few who knew he was adapting his history cards to a book format.

We discussed some of the problems he would run across, and I provided photographs when he needed them. But since our conversations were always via email or phone, I didn't realize just how much his health was declining or I would have asked a lot more questions. Sadly, I did not get a chance for that conversation. The next message I received about Ken was from his friend and neighbor, Frances Roads. After she gave me the sad news that Ken had passed, she put me in touch with the executor of his estate. Frances played a major role in bringing me up to date on Ken's final years and helping me put some of the pieces together on what Ken wanted to be done with his *Hamner* collections and why.

Ken had gathered much more *Hamner* information, photographs, and other documents than we ever imagined. Luckily for the USS *Hamner* (DD-718) Association, Ken left all of this treasure to us.

With the manuscript and Ken's *Hamner* documents and photographs, how did that motivate me to become his editor? My career before retirement had kept me on university campuses both as an employee and a student, leading to three degrees and significant experience in writing, auditing, and editing in addition to my accounting and compliance duties. My photography experience provides me with the skills and equipment needed for the technical parts of the edit. I have spent many hours scanning and photographing records, documents, and memorabilia the association received from Ken's estate in March of 2022.

Was Ken a professional historian, novelist, or biographer? No. But what Ken lacked in his writing background, he more than made up as a detail-oriented and dedicated veteran who wanted us all to learn the dramatic story of the *Hamner* and her crew, in peace and war. He would be happy to know his dream of this book has become a reality. That is why I was willing to do this—for Ken, who served us for so long, and for all of the shipmates who served on the *Hamner*.

Ken's love of the Navy and of the *Hamner* and her crew is shown throughout the book and in his dedication over many years in gathering the information for it. In his writing, Ken shows the human elements of a destroyer and how friendships form during those long months at sea. As I reviewed the text and verified information using the deck logs and other documents, I realized how much he was determined to get these stories out to the public so they would understand what these young men went through and why so many loved the USS *Hamner*.

Throughout the editing process, I did my best to stay true to Ken's original manuscript. Some content was added, but it came from Ken's personal notes, and I feel he would be happy with the few additions. All other edits were grammatical or technical and did not change Ken's story. I have tried to include as many photos and maps as possible to illustrate each chapter. Photographs of shipmates are scattered through the book in addition to content-related photos, and I wish I could have included more. A glossary has been added to help those who are not familiar with all the acronyms and Navy terms.

My hope is that you will enjoy this book as much as I enjoyed helping to complete it. The shipmates of the USS *Hamner* (DD-718) have become part of my family, and I dedicate my work as editor to all of those men.

As always, there are many people to thank when working on a book or any other major project. And although I am sure I will forget someone, let me try to express my appreciation to all who helped me finish this book for Ken.

First of all, I would like to thank my husband, Merrill, for all the dinners he has cooked for us, his editing of my writing, the many sodas he brought to me, the research he helped me with, the Navy books he shared, the copy of *The Chicago Manual of Style* he gave me, and his moral support every step of the way. I thank our dog, Brandon, who has patiently sat by my side as I worked long hours at my desk.

Thank you to the following for going above and beyond to help me finish this dream of Ken's, Frances Roads, Rick Hurd, Matthew Luedke, and Maryellen Arendash.

I would also like to thank the association's board members who have supported my work before, during, and after the work on this book: Nelson Custer, Steve Smith, James Cadden, James Hall, and Jackie Richter.

I have tried to remember everyone who provided photographs, articles, answers to queries from me, and more stories that I was able to add. Please know that I appreciate the support I receive from all of the members of the association and especially Robert O'Malley,

Marc McConahy, Del Mancuso, Glenn Vienna, John Everett, Billy Odle, Paul Esswein, Frank Magistro, Carl Martin, Bill Miller, Gayle Fletcher, Nancy Sicotte, Jon Newcomer, Daryl Patrick, Ashley Gray, William Golder, Robert Frey, Joan Beck, Jimmy Tighe, and Duane Rose.

PREFACE

I have asked myself many times over, what drives one in an endless effort to write this book? I never came up with an answer other than pride. In the beginning, I had no idea it would take so long, for had I realized how long, I may never have attempted to write the book. In essence, this book is the culmination of nearly thirty years of collecting information from her crew, Naval logs stored at the National Archives in College Park, Maryland, and documents and letters from Henry R. Hamner's family. Without these, the book would not have been possible.

Unlike the writing of most books which have a beginning, middle, and end, this book was compiled incrementally over numerous years as the data and photographs were made available to me. I created brochures with this information that were given out each year at reunions held by USS *Hamner* DD-718 Association since 1992.

Naval combat ships such as *Hamner* were in essence weapon platforms employing a crew of young sailors, mostly under the age of twenty-two. During the *Hamner's* life, thousands of sailors crossed her decks, but not one was killed during combat. However, some eleven sailors lost their lives in accidents.

All that being said, this is the story of an American destroyer, USS *Hamner* (DD-718), and her service in major wars and as a training vessel during peacetime. It's also the story of the men who served aboard and knew her well. I dedicate this book to those brave sailors.

I would like to acknowledge the editorial cooperation of Page Publishing, Conneaut Lake, Pennsylvania. I also acknowledge my late wife, Evelyn Ericksen, for her endless efforts without which this book would have never come into existence.

Introduction to the Man Behind This Book

Kenneth Ericksen was born in Spokane, Washington, on March 2, 1932, to Erick and Evelyn Ericksen. Ken grew up with five siblings: his twin brother, Keith; sisters Anna Mae Ericksen and Modelle Radford; and brothers Russell and Patrick.

In 1952, during the Korean War, at the age of twenty, Ken joined the United States Navy on a four-year enlistment. After serving briefly in the Aleutian Islands in the Pacific, Ken was ordered to serve on the USS *Hamner* (DD-718) in 1953 and remained aboard until 1956. Ken then was released from active duty and served four years in the Naval reserves. After he received an honorable discharge in 1960, Ken married Evelyn Holm later that year, and they lived in San Diego, California, the *Hamner*'s homeport. Ken had a long career working for the Department of Defense in San Diego in various positions. Ken also attended National University, earning a master's degree in business. Ken and Evelyn spent their final years in Hayden, Idaho, after Ken retired from the federal government.

As a naval historian and former president of the San Diego Maritime Research Society, Ken gave numerous lectures aboard the Star of India in San Diego, describing life aboard a destroyer and U.S. Naval history, such as Lt. Charles Wilkes' participation in the United States Exploring Expedition of 1846 and its aftermath. He also published articles on Lt. Wilkes.

Ken became a pilot and joined the Civil Air Patrol. He wrote a children's story on flying and created displays of planes and their flights. Ken's twin brother, Keith, was also a member of the Civil Air Patrol.

In 1992, the USS *Hamner* (DD-718) Association was established by a voluntary group of shipmates. Ken supported and participated in the association from the beginning, arriving at the first reunion in Idaho in his white VW "Bug" with "USS *Hamner* DD-718 1953-56" painted in large letters across its back hood. From 1992 until his death, Ken was a charter member and served as historian for the association. As of this writing, Ken holds the record for the number of annual reunions of the association which he attended consecutively (twenty-one) and the total number attended (twenty-two) by a member. In 1996, Ken was awarded a commendation from the association's president for his dedicated service as historian. That dedication would continue until he passed away in 2021.

During his time as historian for the association, Ken collected an abundance of information about the *Hamner* from shipmates, Naval resources, the U.S. Archives in Maryland, and the family of Lt. Henry Rawlings, after whom the ship was named. With this collection of data and photographs, Ken began writing the history of the *Hamner* and transcribed most of those pages into a set of history cards he personally created, printed, and distributed to all of the shipmates he met at the association's annual reunions. The first time many shipmates met Ken, he would tell them he had something to give them and hand them a set of cards with a smile.

At each reunion, Ken led his shipmates in singing his favorite Naval song, "Anchors Aweigh." He would pass out the sheet music and turn on his CD player, and everyone would join in song. The association continues this tradition of singing "Anchors Aweigh" at reunions, in Ken's honor.

Ken's generosity did not stop with these efforts; he also frequently treated his shipmates and guests to special events at reunions linked to his favorite subject, US Naval history. In 2010, Ken provided a catered reception on the liberty ship the SS *Jeremiah O'Brien* at Pier 45 in San Francisco, California. This was a memorable event for all who attended. Ken was a perfectionist—he made sure that even the wine glasses were just what he wanted—bought just for this one event. Four years later, he again treated his fellow shipmates to lunch served in the crew's mess on the USS *Turner Joy* (DD-951) in Bremerton, Washington. This was the last reunion Ken was able to attend, due to his deteriorating health

Ken passed away on October 12, 2021, leaving his love of the *Hamner*, her crew, and her history in this book. His shipmates, their families, and friends who came to know and love this man miss him dearly.

Naval Training 1952, Wedding 1960, First Reunion 1992

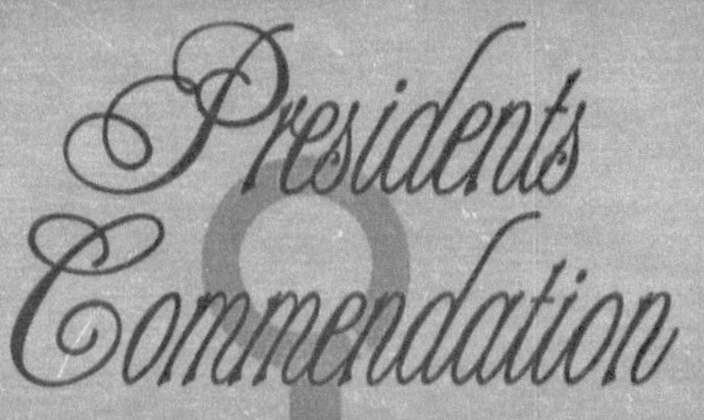
Presidents
Commendation

Presented to

KENNETH ERICKSEN

SHIP'S HISTORIAN

For Exemplary Dedication
To His Ship,
Shipmates and the
United States Navy

U.S.S. HAMNER (DD-718)
Reunion Association
October 1996

Anchors Aweigh led by Past President (Cecil Drewry)
of USS Hamner Association and Ken Ericksen

18th Annual Reunion 2009

Neptunus Rex

Neptune Rex rules the sea
Where he be, I never want to be
I avoid his helm for fear of the sea
I don't want to be shellback-
strong like a porpoise at sea
I live my life as a pollywog at sea
Where Neptune Rex rules the sea
I am who I want to be
A pollywog at sea

—Kenneth Ericksen

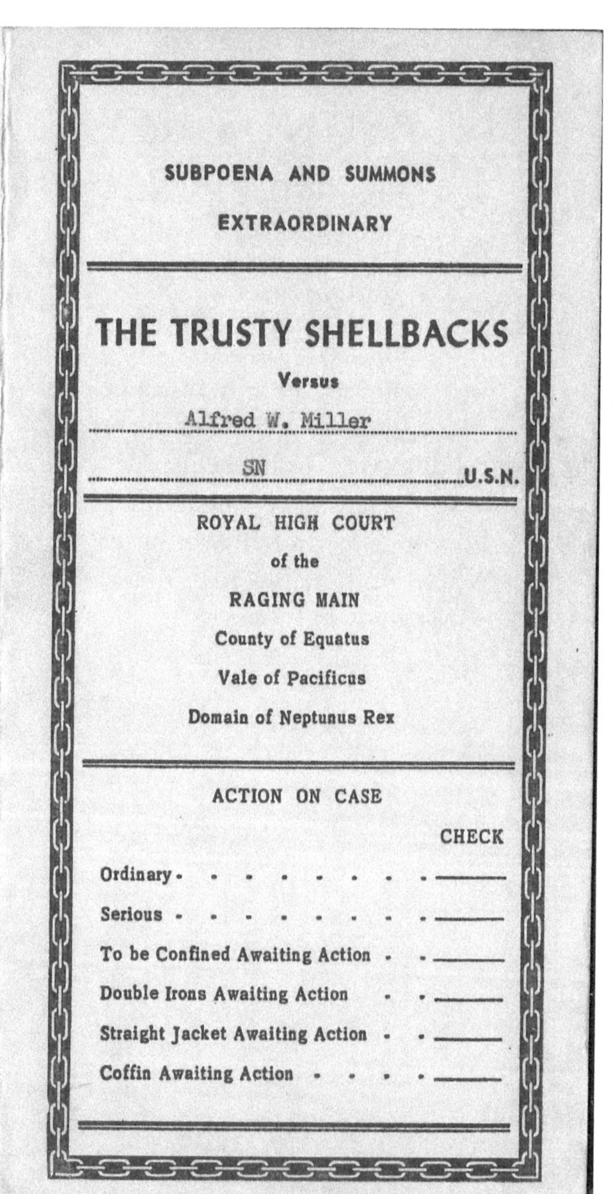

Supoena and Summons

SUBPOENA and SUMMONS EXTRAORDINARY

The Royal High Court of the Raging Main

County of EQUATIS,   )
      Vale of Pacificus,) s. s.
Domain of Neptunus Rex.)

To Whom May Come These Presents:

GREETINGS AND BEWARE

WHEREAS, The good ship _______ HAMNER (DD 718) _______________

bound _____ for AUCKLAND, NEW ZEALAND _________________ is about to enter our domain, and the aforesaid ship carries a large and slimy cargo of land-lubbers, beach-combers, cargo-rats, sea-lawyers, lounge-lizards, parlor dunnigans, plow-deserters, park-bench warmers, chicken-chasers, hay-tossers, sand-crabs, four-flushers, cross-word puzzle bugs and all other living creatures of the land, and last but not least, he-vamps, liberty-hounds and Drug Store cow-boys falsely masquerading as seamen and man-o'-warsmen of which you are a member, having never appeared before us; and

WHEREAS, the Royal High Court of the Raging Main has been convened by us on board of the good ship _______ HAMNER _______ on the _____ 21st _____ day of SEPTEMBER _________ at Longitude ______ 165-47W ____ and Latitude 0°0'0", and an inspection of our Royal High Roster shows that it is high time the sad and wandering nautical soul of that much abused body of yours appeared before the High Tribunal of Neptune; and

BE IT KNOWN, That we hereby summons and command you _____ Alfred W. Miller

_____________________ now a _______ SN ____________________, U.S.N., to appear before the Royal High Court and Our August Presence on the aforesaid date at such time as may best suit our pleasure, and to accept most heartily and with a good grace the pains and penalties of the awful tortures that will be inflicted upon you for daring to enter our aqueous and equinoctial regions without due and submissive ceremony to be examined as to fitness to become one of our Trusty Shellbacks, and a worthy Son of the Sea and answer to the following charges:

CHARGE I. In that ______ Alfred W. Miller

now a _______ SN ____________________, U.S.N., has hitherto willfully and maliciously failed to show reverence and allegiance to our Royal Person, and is therein and thereby a vile land-lubber and pollywog.

CHARGE II, By his constant disturbing Neptunus Rex's nooner with his constant chipping and scrapping.

CHARGE III, ___________________________________

DISOBEY THIS SUMMONS UNDER PAIN OF OUR SWIFT AND TERRIBLE DISPLEASURE. OUR VIGILANCE IS EVER WAKEFUL, OUR VENGEANCE IS JUST AND SURE ! ! !

Given under our hand and seal.

Attest, for the King:
  DAVY JONES, Scribe.

NEPTUNUS REX.

The Charges

1949

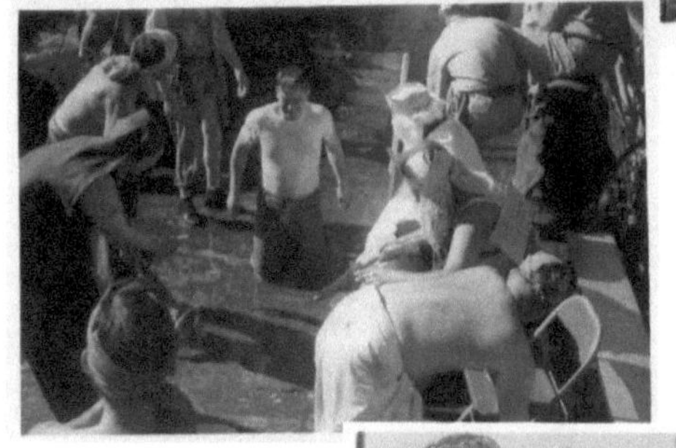

Pollywogs meet King Neptune

...and Davy Jones

1949 Crossing the Equator

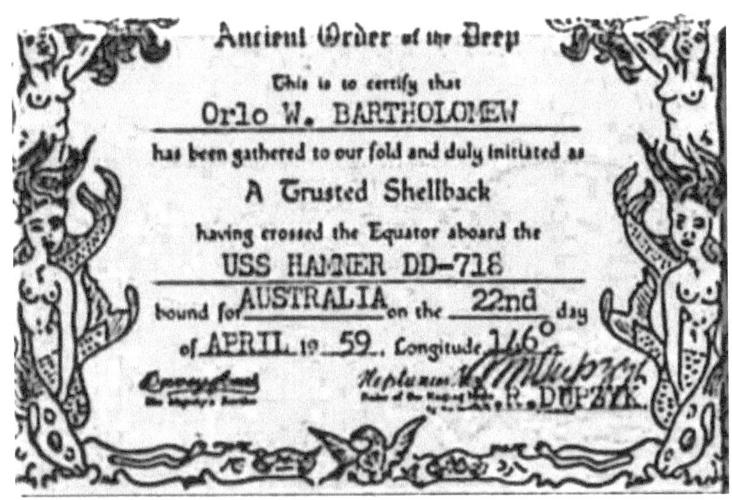

Shellback Certifications

```
************************************************************
```



```
************************************************************
```

THE TORTOISE AND THE LIZARD

There was once a race between a flashy upstart lizard
and a giant sea tortoise. Now the flashy upstart made
loud claims
    "I can beat you anytime," he yelled. "I'm the fastest
thing in the sea."

Lo the time came for the great race. Off they went, the
flashy upstart lizard, swimming for all he was worth,
quickly pulled ahead of the wise old tortoise who was
leisurely taking his time.

A few days later the lizard saw ahead of him the finish
line, above which was a large sign "Welcome to the Equator
and the Realm of King Neptunus Rex." Just before the
lizard was able to speed across the line he was grabbed
by some handsome and powerful sea creatures who began to
beat him mercilessly. After he had swallowed his fourth
helping of garbage the lizard pleaded for mercy.
    "Please, please stop," he cried.
    "I regret that only his Majesty, King Neptune can order
a halt to these festivities," replied one of the creatures,
"and he won't be here for days."

Two days later the tortoise appeared on the scene and
calmly swam across the finish line whereupon he changed
miraculously into King Neptune. Upon seeing the badly
battered lizard, who was still being subjected to the
tortures of the Royal Court, the King ordered a halt to
the activities of his followers and permitted the
lizard to cross the line. Immediately the lizard was
transformed into a handsome sea creature and admitted to
the Royal Court, and to this day he is a loyal follower of
King Neptune.

Moral: He who tries to beat King Neptune at his own game
        shall be subjected to excruciating pain.

The Turtle Times (Shellbacks' Retaliation to Pollywogs' Newsletter)

THE POLLYWOG PRESS

F L A S H   F L A S H   F L A S H

Immediately after the first printing of the Pollywog Press (VOL. I, NO. 1), the scourge of the sea (Shellbacks) immediately took action in the form of their own cheaply imitative newspaper, the "Turtle Times".

In this edition, these ridiculously feeble-minded minnows published a "call-to-arms". Also listed were cruel and unusual punishments to be imposed.

Are we to let this happen? NO! Fellow Pollywogs, I beseech you: UNITE!! Meet brute force with brute force. Meet dim-witted insults with an intellectual prowess far more superior than those weak hypocritical minds can conjure!

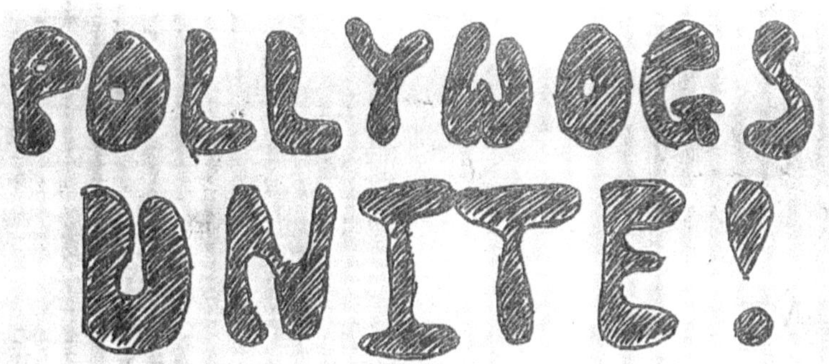

The Pollywog Press

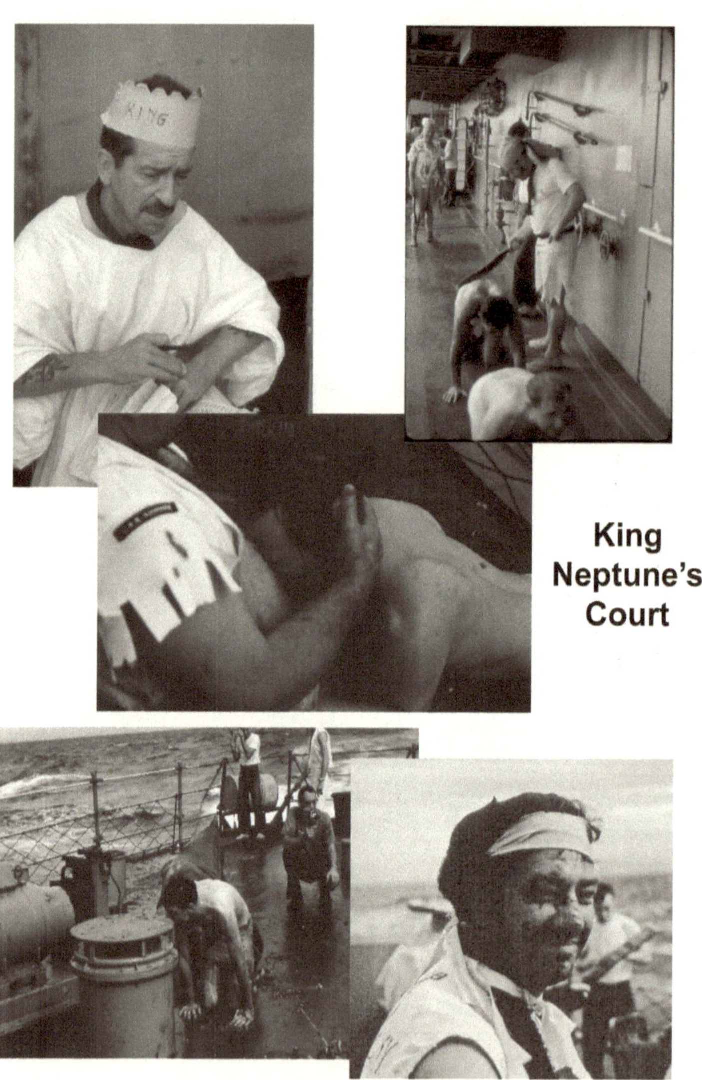

King Neptune's Court—Crossing the Equator

SPECIAL MENU

CROSSING THE EQUATOR

Aboard

Date

Latitude: 00°- 00'

Longitude

☆

SHELLBACKS

Salad Bar	Assorted Bread	Butter
Assorted Dressing		Vegetable Soup
	Griddle Rib Steak	
Francania Potatoes		Mushroom Gravy
French Fries		Green Style Corn
		Buttered Green Beans

Chocolate Layer Cake with White Coconut Icing

Iced Fruit Punch   Hot Fresh Coffee

Complimentary: MARINE PHOTO & PUBLISHING CO.,
P.O. BOX 425, SPRING VALLEY, CALIF. 92077

POLLIWOGS

Assorted Sea Crater Salad	Blood Of The Red Eyed Sea Dog (Tomato Juice with hot sauce)
Scolloped Shark Meat	Flying Fish Wings
Boiled Sea Worms	Boiled Sea Weed
Raw Oysters	with Sowbelly

Sea Weed Au Jus
(Cold Spaghetti with green food coloring)

Jelly Fish Sandwiches

Sea Foam Topping	
Fish Eye Pudding	Hardtack
Last Friday's Left Over Coffee	Brine Water

Note: In the event of a weak stomach, entrée may be
altered only by order of his Majesty King Neptune.

Equator Crossing Menu

CHAPTER 1

Lt. Henry R. Hamner II

The USS *Hamner* (DD-718) was the namesake of Henry R. Hamner II, who was born on March 13, 1922, in London, England. "Pete" was the son of Edward Chambers Hamner Jr. and Dorothy Whitney Kirk. The young Lt. Hamner was named after his uncle, Henry Rawlings Hamner of Fairmont, West Virginia. His father, Commander E. C. Hamner, was the Assistant Naval Attache in London at the time of Henry's birth. Commander E. C. Hamner was later stationed in Honolulu, Hawaii, where Henry's younger sister, Joan Kirk Hamner, was born in 1925. The family had moved back to Lynchburg, Virginia, by 1930, where Henry attended E. C. Glass High School, Class of 1939. In his school yearbook, *The Critic Crest*, Henry appears frequently. He was elected Most Popular Boy in 1939. Beside his name is a long list of activities and groups: National Honor Society; Honor League: Varsity Club; Track '37, Manager, '38; Football, '37; Senior Council; Pres., Hi-Y Club, '39; Junior Class Pres; Senior Class Pres.; Athletic Association; and Spanish Club.

After graduation from high school, Henry was appointed to the US Naval Academy, Class of 1943. In his final year at the academy, Hamner was in the 15th Company and graduated one year ahead of schedule because of WW II, when he was commissioned an ensign. Henry then served as an instructor at Harvard University's Naval Training School during the summer of 1942 until he was ordered to the Service Force, Atlantic Subordinate Command, Naval Base,

Norfolk, Virginia. While in Norfolk, Ensign Henry R. Hamner and Miss Elsie McDowell Jackson were married on November 2, 1942.

On May 1, 1943, Hamner was promoted to lieutenant (junior grade). He was then ordered to Bethlehem Steel Company in New York, where he was on duty fitting out on the USS *Daly* (DD-519), and then served on her after her commissioning. Henry Hamner (known as Junior on the *Daly*), was now a *plank owner*. In Henry's letters to his mother, he told her of how impressed he was with the *Daly* and her crew. Henry received a telegram from the Red Cross while on the *Daly*. Hamner's son, Peter Clay Hamner, had been born on August 20, 1943.

A transfer from the *Daly* to the USS *Howorth* (DD-592) pre-commissioning crew made Henry a plank owner again. Hamner was promoted to full lieutenant in July 1944 on board the *Howorth*). By August 1944, the ship was on her way to join the Seventh Fleet in the pacific.

Aboard the *Howorth*, Lt. Hamner (known as Pete by his shipmates), supported the Morotai landings, the Western New Guinea campaigns, the Philippine liberation, and the *Iwo Jima* invasion.

On March 11, 1945, Lt. and Mrs. Hamner's second child, Susan McDowell Hamner, was born. Only three weeks later, *Howorth* arrived at Okinawa on April 1, 1945. On April 6, in a desperate attempt to prevent total defeat for Japan, the first of ten massed Japanese kamikaze aircraft attacks began against the U.S. Navy and British aircraft carrier task force screening American combat forces landed on Okinawa Island. The kamikaze aircraft struck fear in every sailor in the fleet. During the onslaught, in which three destroyers, an LST, and two ammunitions ships were sunk plus ten others damaged, six kamikaze planes attacked the Howorth. While manning his battle station in the gun fire control director located atop the pilot house, Lt. Hamner, as gunnery officer, directed his fire to shoot down five of the attacking planes. The sixth crashed directly into the gun director. Lt. Hamner, along with eight crewmen, lost his life. His last words were "Target angle zero," indicating the kamikaze was heading straight for the gun director. At age twenty-three, Lt. Hamner was posthumously awarded the Silver Star for gallantry in action, and he is buried at Arlington National Cemetery, Virginia.

The ship, USS *Hamner* (DD-718), came to life when she was authorized for construction on July 9, 1942. After being given the name Henry Rawlings Hamner, the long-hulled Gearing-class destroyer was launched on November 24, 1945, by the Federal Ship Building and Drydock Co., Port Newark, New Jersey, and she was christened by Mrs. Henry Rawlings Hamner (widow of Lt. Hamner). The new destroyer was primarily designed as an anti-submarine-warfare (ASW) ship but could fulfil a wide variety of combat roles, including defense against enemy warships and aircraft reconnaissance and naval gunfire support for ground troops. *Hamner* was one of ninety-eight such vessels built for the Department of the Navy between 1942 and 1952. Those years define the Gearing-class destroyers and the crews who served on them.

Now the story of the USS *Hamner* (DD-718) and her crews can be told.

Henry Hamner, US Naval Academy, 15th Company, 1942

USS Daly (DD-519), First ship on which Ensign Hamner served

Ensign Henry Rawlings Hamner II

USS Howorth (DD-592) where Lt. Hamner was KIA on April 6, 1945

CHAPTER 2

Now Hear This—All Hands Turn to 1946–1949

Born as a result of the tide of history at the time, the USS *Hamner* (DD-718) was commissioned July 12, 1946. After completing postcommissioning shakedown repairs at the Brooklyn Navy Yard, *Hamner* set sail for Port-au-Prince, Haiti, in the Caribbean where her crew went ashore for liberty before proceeding through the Panama Canal to her future home port, San Diego, California. Here she joined Squadron 11, Destroyer Division 111, comprised of sister ships USS *Chandler* (DD717), *Ozbourn* (DD-846), and *Wiltsie* (DD-716).

As her first crew learned (as did all the future crews), life aboard the new destroyer was uncomfortable, to say the least. Quarters were cramped for some 230 men who served aboard (or any other class destroyer for that matter). Constant duty and a lack of the comforts enjoyed on larger ships made living conditions difficult. Heavy seas tossed the ship mercilessly, drenching the crew and interior with salt water. Eating in the galley during these times was difficult, hanging on to the tray or flatware. "Tin Can Sailor" was the distinguishing mark of a destroyer man!

On December 9, 1946, as her crew watched a late evening movie (*Gone with the Wind*) on the fantail in San Diego Bay, a smoldering cigar butt was inadvertently placed on a 16mm film magazine carrier sitting between depth charges. "General Quarters, General Quarters! All hands man your battle stations, this is not a drill," (as the film went up in explosive flames). That night was *Hamner's* first threatening drill (one of many she was to experience throughout her life).

Departing San Diego in January 1947, the destroyer steamed for the Far East on her first WestPac cruise (she made eighteen such cruises in her life), stopping on the way at Hawaii and Midway Island, and the port city of Yokohama where she replenished while en route to Sasebo, Japan. At the time, Japan was under post-war occupation by American armed forces, and Sasebo, although still damaged from WWII, was the most accessible logistic center for the Seventh Fleet. *Hamner* was next assigned to operations out of Tsingtao, China, with the Asiatic Fleet.

By early March as Nationalist China's government was clashing with Communist forces in the Chinese Civil War, *Hamner* received orders to make a flank speedrun from Tsingtao to Chen Chow-Wae (where the Great Wall meets the ocean) to support the evacuation of a US Marine detachment caught between opposing forces. Upon the successful evacuation of the Marines by an LST (Landing Ship Tank), which later placed the Marines aboard a merchant vessel in the bitter cold of night, the destroyer returned to Tsingtao, China, with the Asiatic Fleet.

Navigating up the Yangtze River, then to the Huangpu River, the destroyer on Easter Sunday that year made her first visit to the city of Shanghai. Mooring midstream near the heart of the city, her crew experienced seeing one of the great cities of the world trying to rebuild from the results of WWII, as distant artillery fire between Nationalist government troops and Communist forces could be heard.

Returning stateside in September, *Hamner* operated out of San Diego until March of 1948, at which time she proceeded to Bremerton, Washington, for yard overhaul. Having completed sea trials on June 28, she next steamed to Port Angeles, Washington, where her crew celebrated the Fourth of July, thereafter returning to San Diego, August 5, 1948.

After completing a series of underway training exercises at San Diego, the destroyer on September 17 entered the Long Beach Naval Shipyard facility in California. Here she underwent dry-dock repairs involving a split seam, as she made final preparations for her upcoming WestPac cruise.

In early October, the destroyer (in company with DesDiv-111) departed for the Far East, rendezvousing with Task Force 38 en route to the Orient and deployment with the Seventh Fleet. On November 24, 1948, while engaged in Hunter-Killer night operation off Tsingtao, it witnessed the collision between the *Chandler* and *Ozbourn*, resulting in the death of two *Ozbourn* sailors. The badly damaged *Ozbourn* was replaced in the squadron by the USS *Chevalier* (DD-805).

As the first week of December 1948 drew to a close, *Hamner* found herself berthed at wharf number two in Tsingtao. Here she received urgent orders to proceed north to the city of Tanghu (near Peking) where an anchored American merchant vessel off-loading cargo was fearful of coming under attack by Communist forces. Arriving late at night, along with the cruisers *Springfield* (CL-66) and *St. Paul* (CA-73), *Hamner* with crew ready at battle station shined a bright light on both her flag and that of the merchant vessel. For five long days, in bitter cold weather, with Communist shore lights blinking "Americans get out," *Hamner* held her battle station ready. On the fifth night, as the sound of gunfire surrounded the destroyer and flashes lit the night skies, it escorted the merchant ship to safe ocean passage.

In need of upkeep and maintenance, *Hamner* returned to Tsingtao on December 16, 1948. She tied alongside the destroyer tender USS *Sierra* (AD-18) for fifteen days. Having celebrated Christmas and the New Year at Tsingtao (a wild town), the destroyer, on January 15, 1949, hoisted anchor to prepare to sail to Shanghai, then on to Keelung, Taiwan, for a short stay. "Boatswain, this is the captain. Haul in the gangplank, make preparations to be underway for Hong Kong."

"Captain Sleight! We can't find our dog, Lady.[1] She is not aboard, sir."

"Belay that order, send a search party ashore. We can't sail without our mascot." Upon locating Lady, *Hamner* sailed for Hong Kong where her crew enjoyed a few good days of liberty before steaming to Taipei, Taiwan, prior to retuning to Tsingtao.

Operating in the Yellow Sea throughout the months of February and March, including numerous refueling stops at Buckner Bay, Okinawa, *Hamner*, in March 1949, found herself anchored at the mouth of the Yung-Ting Ho Canal at Tientsin, waiting for Chinese diplomats to board for safe passage to Taiwan. As the civil war raged between Nationalist and Communist forces, her crew waited and watched gunfire light the night skies. By morning, the diplomats had not shown, and with the situation growing extremely tense by the hour, *Hamner* soon left for Tsingtao.

By April 20, 1949, *Hamner* was once again back in Woosung (down the river five miles southeast of Shanghai). Here wire radio dispatches reaching *Hamner* by a navy motor whaleboat from the light cruiser *Pasadena* (CL-65) warned that the British sloop [destroyer escort] *Amethyst*, while en route to supply the British Embassy in Nanking a day earlier, had come under fire by Communist guns some sixty-five miles east of the city of Yangtze. This action resulted in three dead and twenty wounded sailors. The dispatch went on to read that the British sloop *Consort* had been sent from Shanghai to help. However, as she attempted under fire to run the gauntlet that morning, some eighty four-inch field guns massed on the river bank and she was forced to return when her steering gear was damaged from an artillery hit. Also, that morning, two other British warships (the sloop *Black Swan* and the cruiser *London*) which had been sent to assist, had broken through the gauntlet without incident, and

---

[1] In May 1949, upon *Hamner*'s departure from Japan for the States, her mascot Lady was left with sailors stationed at the Yokosuka Naval base where it gave birth to a batch of pups.

were escorting the *Amethyst* to Shanghai, indicating they would fight their way back if required.[2]

Another dispatch reaching *Hamner* by morning's end indicated the British admiralty in London had ordered the cruiser *Belfast* (with armor capable of withstanding direct six-inch shell hits), and the 1,710-ton sloop *Constance* to rush to Shanghai from Hong Kong. Also, the American hospital ship USS *Repose* (AH-16) had been placed at British disposal and was rushing from Tsingtao.

That evening at 1900, the *Consort* returned, berthing Pootung on the Huangpu river (a branch of the Yangtze) across from Shanghai, reporting battle casualties aboard at twenty-seven dead, and three wounded.

The next morning as the *Repose* arrived and was standing off Woosung to assist the British with their casualties, news reached *Hamner* that Communist gunners shelled two more British ships on the river, boosting casualties to forty-three killed and eighty wounded in two days of fighting. In addition, the American mission in Nanking, including most of the Marine guard for the embassy, was being flown out to Shanghai.

As international complications to the explosive Far East situation grew, British and American naval authorities met to decide whether all foreign warships should be withdrawn from the Yangtze river. During these very trying days in China, *Hamner* and her crew stood duty-ready to carry out any mission ordered by the State Department.

Hamner's last operation in war-torn China occurred May 5, 1949, when she steamed up the Yangtze and Huangpu Rivers to the city of Woosung. Here she evacuated Nationalist Chinese diplomats, their wives and children as Communist gunfire surrounded the city. With artillery fire splashing throughout the river basin, the destroyer departed the war-torn city and steamed to Yokosuka, Japan, where, on May 20, the diplomats disembarked. Upon completing the oper-

---

[2] In 1950, the British made a movie about the *Amethyst* incident named *Battle Hell*. More information on the many films and books on the incident can be found by searching the web for the Yangtze Incident and the HMS *Amethyst*.

ation, *Hamner* soon departed for the States, stopping at Pearl Harbor (four hours of liberty was granted during refueling), while en route to San Diego, arriving June 4, 1949.

Shortly after her arrival home as the Nationalist government on mainland China fell, the crew learned that flashing signal messages in Shanghai had warned all foreign warships they had twenty-four hours to get out of the country, or they would be blown out of the water.

Having previously made arrangements involving future training exercises in San Francisco, *Hamner* soon departed San Diego steaming north for the port city. As her crew looked up, the destroyer passed beneath the Golden Gate Bridge for the first time on June 26, 1949. Upon completion of numerous training exercises in the area, she returned to San Diego on July 10.

By August 2, 1949, the destroyer was back in San Francisco where it picked up navy midshipmen for sea training. Shortly thereafter, *Hamner* rendezvoused with the cruisers USS *Toledo* (CA-122) and *Springfield* (CL-66) on a training mission to Balboa, Panama, via the Galapagos Islands and waters off Ecuador, South America.

"Excuse me, Captain Sleight!"

"What can I do for you, midshipman?"

"Sir, I was wondering if I could hide in your cabin. You see, sir, there is this rowdy gang roosting on the fantail, and I don't want anything to do with them!"

"Sailor, not even the almighty power of a sea captain can avoid them."

On August 12, 1949, as *Hamner* crossed the equator at longitude 91-45W and latitude 000 degrees off South America (her first crossing of many), Neptunus Rex and his goon squad ravaged every space in the destroyer, seeking out her slimy cargo of pollywogs, liberty hounds, plow deserters, and drugstore cowboys masquerading as destroyer men. By day's end, not only had the destroyer become shellback-strong, so had her crew.

Steaming Northwest, *Hamner* arrived back in San Diego on August 31, and shortly thereafter, proceeded to Long Beach, arriving September 3. By September 13, she was again in San Francisco, where she off-loaded all midshipmen and took aboard a new bunch before setting sail for Hawaii and training exercises in and around the islands lasting throughout the month of October and into November. In early December 1949, the destroyer returned to the States, arriving at Mare Island Naval Shipyard, Vallejo, California, where it commenced a four-month overhaul.

1946
USS Hamner DD-718

U.S.S. HAMNER
(DD-718)
1948

Harvey Hebert 1949

Fred Richter 1946-48

William Murphy 1946-48

Thurman Savell 1946-53

1946 - 1948
USS Wiltsie   USS Chandler   USS Hamner   USS Ozbourn

DD-746 Haussig
DD-718 Hamner
DD-716 Wiltsie

Lady and "her" Crew 1949

Lady at home on the sea

Allen BM3 with
Lady (L)

CHAPTER 3

On the Way—Korea, 1950–1951

As the New Year 1950 rang in at Mare Island Naval Shipyard, Vallejo, California, *Hamner* continued her yard overhaul which began in December the previous year. Here the destroyer was refurbished and equipped with new three-inch/50 mm antiaircraft armament, a tripod mast, and improved radar. Upon completion, *Hamner* arrived back at her home port, San Diego, in March. She then rejoined her sister ships of Squadron 11, Destroyer Division 111, comprised of the USS *Wiltsie* (DD-716), USS *Chandler* (DD-717), and USS *Chevalier* (DDR-805).

Quietly swinging on the hook (buoy) on the morning of June 24, 1950, as her crew watched PBY flying boats take off and land in the harbor, news reached the destroyer that Communist North Korea had attacked the Republic of South Korea (ROK). By day's end, American armed forces were committed to supporting the United Nations in the struggle to protect the ROK, including the Seventh Fleet deployment in the Taiwan Strait to discourage any dangerous escalation of hostilities between Taiwan and China as a result of the conflict.[3]

---

[3] The movement of the Seventh Fleet to protect Formosa (Taiwan) in July 1950 may have angered China more than the decision to provide support for South Korea.

Moving to the Broadway Pier on the twenty-eighth, the destroyer immediately commenced replenishment, and as the sun rose over the harbor the morning of July 6, the word was passed to "make preparation for getting underway." "Captain Hughes! The special sea detail has been set, but we are out of toilet paper. There is none to be found at the naval supply center."

"Sailor, send a work party ashore and buy all you can at the local market, and be sure to save the wrappings on our apples" was the captain's order that morning.

As her crew worked at welding three new 20mm guns (capable of fifty shots with a tracer every seven rounds in one minute) to the fantail, the naval greyhound at 0852, with sister destroyers, quietly slipped past Point Loma, rendezvousing at sea with the heavy cruiser USS *Helena* (CA-75) and her sister ships, forming a task group en route for the Far East, stopping for fuel at Pearl Harbor and again at Midway Island where, under sweltering heat, two hours port and starboard liberty was granted, allowing most crew members just enough time to swim to cool off.

Proceeding in column up Tokyo Bay, the task group arrived in Yokosuka, Japan, on July 21, where they loaded ammunition. By the twenty-third, the task group was underway for Sasebo, arriving at the critical port city on the twenty-fifth, where ships of various units of the United States, British, and Australian Pacific fleet were moored, ready to cross the Korea Strait.

As the sound of water slipped beneath the bow, *Hamner* commenced her first-time war cruise in the early hours of July 26, 1950, when the task group departed Sasebo for nearby Korean waters, until orders sent them steaming south to Taiwan.[4]

Arriving off Taiwan, the task group commenced patrolling the Taiwan Strait (separating the island from mainland China) watching for any suspicious ships. Although *Hamner* investigated numerous contacts, each proved to be a merchant ship carrying on normal

---

[4] The United States ceased regular naval patrols of the Taiwan Strait on January 1, 1979 after relaxation of tensions in the area.

trade. After one week of patrol, the task group was ordered to return to Sasebo on August 3.

Having refueled at the Jasco fuel docks in Sasebo, the destroyer moored alongside the USS *Diachenko* (APD-123) until orders sent her steaming for the eastern coast of Korea on the sixth as part of cruiser Task Group 95.2 to support heavily outnumbered UN troops who were being pushed back toward the southern port city of Pusan. During the onslaught, *Hamner,* at 0311 on the morning of August 7, 1950, fired her first salvo against an enemy, when it commenced firing on railway marshalling yards with the USS *Helena* (CL-50), south of the city Tanchon (seventy miles north of Pusan).

By the ninth of August, having received three members of a Korean naval liaison team by motor whaleboat from the *Helena, Hamner* proceeded to Pusan for refueling. Transferring the Koreans ashore, the destroyer tied alongside the Japanese tanker, *Meisho Maru,* where it received sixty-seven thousand gallons of fuel. Shortly afterward, the Pusan Water Barge Company delivered fifteen thousand gallons of fresh water. At day's end (while her crew looked over the town with binoculars), the destroyer departed, and by 2220, was back firing at enemy truck convoy traffic along coastal roads. By midafternoon on August 11, *Hamner* commenced firing at an enemy tugboat towing three barges, destroying the target, and sinking two smaller boats about one thousand yards offshore.

Working at preventing the advance of North Korean forces in their fierce drive southward, *Hamner* arrived off Yongdok at 0552 on August 14, where it maneuvered seaward of two ROK LSTs supporting troops evacuations ashore. With crew mustered at General Quarters, *Hamner* relayed a message by signal light that she was preparing to commence harassment and interdiction fire including bombardment five miles north and south of Yonchu Kapu. Firing throughout the day and late into the night at sporadic intervals (eight targets on the odd hour and ten on the even hour) with good results, the destroyer steamed back to Yongdok.

Continuing blockade patrol, the destroyer, on August 15, found herself in support efforts to rescue units of the Third ROK Army Division by sea after they had been cut off by enemy forces near Yonghae. On that summer night, the *Helena*, accompanied by *Hamner* and *Wiltsie*, four LSTs, the *DeHaven* (DD-717), and *Arakara* (ATF-98) took station 1,800 yards off Daisain Matsu cove. As flashes of naval gunfire lit the night sky, the LSTs, guided by lights from jeeps ashore, beached, and by daybreak, had rescued some 5,800 troops and over 1,200 civilian evacuees, with no loss of personnel or equipment. On August 17, while escorting the LSTs to Kyulyuho Ko (where the ROK troops relanded), *Hamner* was ordered back to Yongdok where she carried out call fire harassment operations (firing on target every ten minutes) in support of troop evacuations there.

After the successful evacuation at Yongdok the task group returned to Sasebo on August 19 for replenishment and liberty. *Hamner* spent most of her time in and out of Sasebo during the Korean War. Because of Sasebo's location (156 sea miles from Pusan) and its excellent harbor anchorage, port activities there soon eclipsed Yokosuka (located some 500 sea miles further from Korea) as the most accessible logistic center for naval forces. Here, *Hamner's* crew saw various units of the UN-combined *police fleet* for the first time.

By August 24, the destroyer was back off the eastern coast of Korea bombarding enemy shipping and railroad installations in and around Tanchon and the village of Osantoku. By the twenty-seventh, she was off Bayo-to Island, investigating a suspect radar bogey (contact). Here the *Chevalier*, at 0010, commenced illumination fire, as *Hamner*, with her crew, mustered at battle stations, sought target contact, which turned out to be the friendly ROK vessel *YMS-516*. By sunset the following day, the destroyer was laying in swift currents four thousand yards off Taruhan Kutsu (Pohang area), engaged in heavy fire. Using her twin screws to hold position and heading (while rolling the main engines every there minutes to prevent warping), *Hamner* fired at enemy gun positions and troop enhancements late into the night as she assisted in repelling a massive North Korean attack on UN land forces.

On August 31, at 0513, while searching for targets of opportunity, the destroyer received an SOS from the South Korean naval vessel *YMS 308*, which had run aground on rocks off Ko-point. Dispatching her motor whaleboat to investigate, the crew reported back at 0631 that the vessel was badly holed and no assistance was required since lighters were already alongside to unload equipment and crew. Thereafter, *Hamner*, at a distance of 2,800 yards off Choki point and Geijit Wan, continued shore bombardment against enemy targets.

Steaming back to Sasebo from the Pohang area on the first of September (after passing through antisubmarine netting at harbor entrance), she tied up alongside the destroyer tender USS *Dixie* (AD-14), riding at anchor in the channel. Not knowing when she would be called upon again for duty on the battle line, her crew worked around the clock, making the most of allocated maintenance time for tender availability with very little liberty.

By September 11, *Hamner* once again was underway for duty off Korea. However, this time she became one of the screens for carriers of Task Force 77. On September 15, with her crew at battle-ready stations off the west coast of Korea, the course of the Korean War was about to change as the amphibious landing at Inchon, behind enemy lines, began. Within ten days of the UN landing, the North Korean military effort that had reached the very doorstep of Pusan was struggling frantically to reassemble and redeploy for the defense of its own territory north of the 38th parallel where it had begun the invasion months before. After operating in the Yellow Sea through October 4 with the task force, *Hamner* returned to Sasebo.

Departing Sasebo on October 9, the destroyer took station TF-77 for plane guard duty involving the USS *Boxer* (CV-21), *Leyte Gulf* (CV-32), *Valley Forge* (CV-45), *Philippine Sea* (CV-47) and the cruiser *Manchester* (CL-83) off the east coast of Korea. At 1503 on the cold bleak afternoon of October 14, activities were brisk on her bridge as crew members watched returning attack aircraft landings.

"Excuse me, Captain Hughes. A sparrow (bird) has landed on the forecastle."

"Ensign, is this your first battle cruise?"

"Yes, Captain."

"Then, sailor, enter the sighting in the deck log remark sheets, and record the time."

"Aye, aye, Captain."

After twenty-one days at sea, *Hamner* returned to Sasebo on October 30 for fuel. Upon refueling, the destroyer set sail for Yokosuka, arriving on November 2, for yard work. Here her crew (after the disbursing officer returned to the ship with Japanese yen worth US $4,000) enjoyed some well-earned liberty as the destroyer made preparations for returning to the battle line.

At the time, a total UN victory over the North Korean aggressors seemed assured. The North Korean Army was crushed; their divisions were completely routed. Thousands of enemy troops had surrendered, and hundreds more were deserting their arms. Entire North Korean divisions had completely disintegrated over the Korean countryside in disorganized units.

Underway November 6, *Hamner* once again steamed for the east coast of Korea's operation area, and by the tenth, was a part of TF-77, comprised of the USS *Philippine Seas* (CV-47), *Princeton* (CV-37), *Leyte Gulf* (CV-32), Valley *Forge* (CV-45), *Missouri* (BB-63), *St. Paul* (CA-73), *Juneau* (CL-119), *Worchester* (CL-144) and with DesDivs 31, 92, and 111 as escorts.

Operating independently from the task force on November 19, in an area where disabled aircraft could ditch, and their pilots be picked up immediately in the freezing water, *Hamner* spotted a life jacket (covered with oil) observed to have a body in it. Picking up the body, whose only identification painted on the life jacket was "USALT-392," it appeared to be Korean, with no visible wounds and dead, apparently from exposure. Before executing darken ship (1645 hours) and returning to the main body of the task force, service for burial of the dead at sea was held. The captain read the services, and the body was committed to the deep at Lat 39-34.IN, Long 129-17.8E.[5]

Maneuvering to sink two floating mines early on the morning of November 25, a 5/38 AA common projectile exploded prematurely after being fired from mount 52, and fragments of the

---

[5] The body retrieved off Korea on November 19 carried various foreign currencies in large denominations, gold coins, wristwatches, and numerous foreign identification papers.

projectile punctured the forecastle deck, terrifying all hands on the bridge. The explosion was caused by a faulty fuse. That same morning, news reached *Hamner* that Chinese troops had intervened in the war in massive numbers on the side of North Korea without warning and were pushing the UN forces back down the peninsula. Low on fuel at the time, the destroyer returned to Sasebo on the twenty-eighth where she refueled before mooring alongside the USS *Hector* (AR-7) at buoy 16, and immediately took on ammunition and replenishments.

As the UN military forces' situation continued to worsen, *Hamner*, on December 4, was ordered underway for Korea once again. Rendezvousing with TF-77 carriers, the destroyer took station in formation with eighteen destroyers screening the *Princeton, Manchester,* and *Missouri.* Early dispatches reaching the destroyer indicated the Eighth Army was in the most critical condition and needed immediate redeployment. Men of the Eighth Army (tenth Corps) First Marine Division were severely affected, being pushed back by Chinese forces. The ports of Hungnam and Wonsan were selected for withdrawal and evacuation of UN forces from North Korea, and by December 7, out loading of all army and marine stores had commenced.

Radio news dispatches reaching the destroyer at sea on December 24 indicated that virtually all US naval forces in the Far East were now concentrated on the northeast coast off Korea at Hungnam and Wonsan as troops were being withdrawn. With a covering canopy of naval aircraft from TF-77 carriers, plus a steel curtain of shellfire from the naval armada supporting the perimeter, the troops were sealifted to Pusan. This was a massive undertaking, the largest American sealift since the Okinawa campaign of WWII. By January 5, 1951, facilities at both ports in North Korea were destroyed to prevent their use by the enemy, and the ports closed. After operating thirty-three days at sea with the task force, *Hamner* returned to Sasebo on January 7.

By January 18, 1951, *Hamner* again had departed Sasebo, becoming part of TF-77 whose planes were pounding Communist troops. By 1600 on the twenty-second, in bitter cold seas, her crew was sent running to general fire quarters as the main forward engine room electrical panel went up in explosive flames, threatening to burn through bulkheads to fuel tanks. Having extinguished the fire, the crew worked desperately hard at maintaining restored emergency functions of the panel while underway. Directed by dispatch on February 13, *Hamner* proceeded to Yokosuka, where on the fifteenth, it moored at buoy C1 in the outer harbor, and naval yard workers from ashore commenced installing a new panel. Also, newly located and highly classified topographic sounding charts of the Korean coast, made by the Japanese Imperial Navy during WWII, were placed aboard to aid in coastal navigation.

Departing Yokosuka in a blinding snowstorm on February 23, the destroyer, in company of the carrier *Princeton* and her sister ships of DesDiv-111, steamed out of the harbor, heading for operations off Korea with TF-77. At the time, US Army and Marine units were slugging it out in bitter cold on the peninsula against Chinese troops in a military situation that continued to worsen for the UN forces. Although naval air power was cutting the enemy supply lines, the Communists continued to mount pressure. During this period, *Hamner* as escort worked hard in dangerous, rough, ice-cold seas to meet the demands of carriers whose aircraft were pounding enemy position around the clock. On March 10, the destroyer departed TF-77 off the east coast of Korea and steamed for Yokosuka, arriving the eleventh, where she immediately commenced unloading ammunition.

By March 12, *Hamner* was underway from Yokosuka, en route to Hawaii in company of DesDiv-111 (bypassing Midway Island), arriving at Pearl Harbor at 0727, where she commenced refueling. After a search of the ship for possible stowaways, the destroyer was underway for San Diego, California, at 1320.

After nine months of action in the Korean theater, *Hamner* and the battle-weary crew returned to the States, arriving in San Diego at 0726 on March 25, 1951, where she moored alongside the USS *Dixie* (AD-14) at buoy number 21 and 22. It was a great day for her crew.

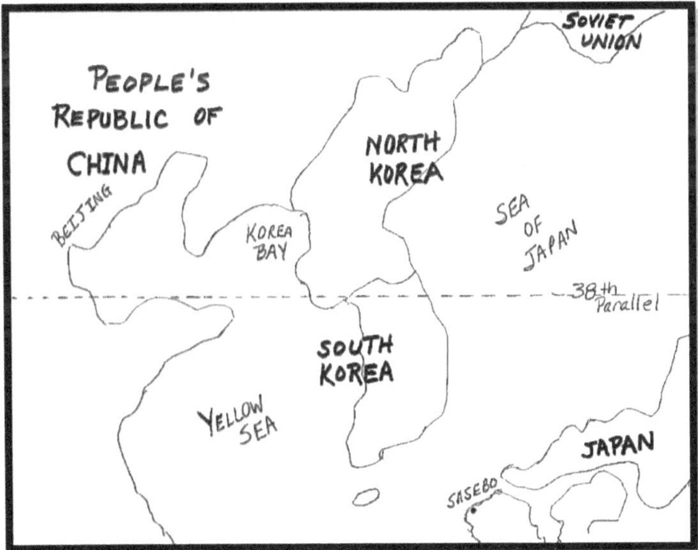

USS Hamner (circa 1950) top / Informal map of Hamner's cruises

Bob O'Malley 1948-51

Billy Odle 1949-55

Ralph Taylor 1948-54

Duane Tucker 1949-52

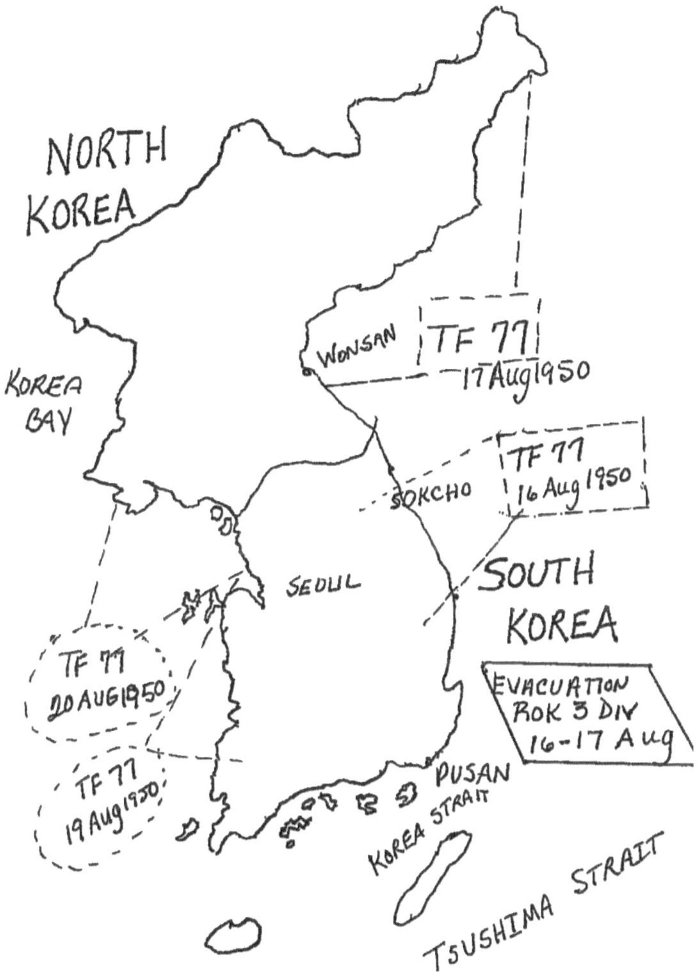

Hamner was with Task Force 77 in August 1950

SHIP OR STATION

U.S.S. HANNER (DD718)

24 January 1951:
Commended at Captain's Mast this date for brave and expeditious action as
Chief Petty Officer in Charge of Repair #2 in entering a burning compartment
amid exploding small arms ammunition and fighting the fire until it was
extinguished, on 22 January 1951.

J. B. HOUGH, LCDR, USN,
Executive Officer.

DATE

NOT
ity i
and
gram

FOR U

SIGNATURE AND RANK

REPOR

NAME (Last)	(First)	(Middle)	SERVICE NO.	BRANCH AND CLASS
MC GUIRE,	William	Finch	375 98 71	USN

Bill McGuire commendation by captain 1951

Yokosuka 1951: O'Malley (4th from left),
Kabachinski, ships baker (3rd from right)

CHAPTER 4

The Siege of Wonsan, 1951–1953

Having arrived in San Diego from Korea in March 1951, with her sister ships of Squadron 11 Division 111, comprised of the USS *Wiltsie* (DD-716), *Theodore E. Chandler* (DD-717), and the *Chevalier* (DDR-805), *Hamner*, after a short stand-down for crew shore leave, commenced making preparation for her upcoming fourth WestPac cruise. Entering Long Beach Naval Shipyard (Terminal Island) in July, the destroyer underwent an upgrade involving the aft mount 33 (5"/38) and new ASW ordinance. Thereafter, for the next six months, *Hamner* engaged in various training exercises and fleet maneuvers off San Diego and San Clemente Island.

Departing for the Korean Theater with her sister ships of Squadron 11 Division on 15 October 1951, the destroyer steamed past Point Loma, setting a course for Japan via Honolulu and Midway Island. Arriving Yokosuka on November 6, *Hamner* took on ammunitions, and on the thirteenth, departed in company with the USS *Essex* (CV-9) for Task Force 77, in Korean waters.

On the decks of the *Hamner*, ready for immediate use, were grenades and submachine guns to counter the threat that Communist troops might come out from the shore and attempt to board in the event the destroyer became disabled by a mine, or became grounded near a hostile coast.

Arriving in waters off the east coast of Korea on November 17, *Hamner* assumed a position as screening destroyer for the carrier USS

Bon Homme Richard (CV-31), the battleship *Wisconsin* (BB-64), and the cruisers *Los Angeles* (CA-135) and *St. Paul* (CA-73). Detached from screen activities five days later, the destroyer commenced providing independent shore bombardment for Korean ground troops in the vicinity of Wonsan. During this time, she observed a plane crash bearing some five miles distant. As she sped at twenty-five knots (247 rpm) to render assistance, *Hamner* was informed that the pilot had been picked up by an LSM and that screen assistance would be needed during transfer of the pilot to the cruiser *Los Angeles*. Upon assisting in the transfer, the destroyer returned to her patrol station where she conducted shore bombardment and screening activities until the first week of December. Leaving the fighting zone on December 7 in weather exceptionally rough (fifteen-foot to twenty-foot seas), the destroyer steamed for Sasebo, Japan, where she moored for maintenance and shore leave over the holidays. By January 8, 1952, she once again was underway, maneuvering through Sasebo's harbor and anti-submarine nets, en route in winter conditions to rejoin the task force.

Winter in Korean waters brought chill and biting Siberian winds, heavy seas, and subzero temperatures to the destroyer and her sister ships. *Hamner's* superstructure was often sheathed in ice, locking the forward mounts in azimuth and freezing depth charges in their racks. The icy wind had such a razor bite to the crew's faces and hands that refueling and replenishment often took place on a downwind bearing.

By the ninth, the destroyer was again maneuvering on various courses and speeds, operating with the cruiser *St. Paul*, delivering harassment and interdiction (H&I) fire at prearranged targets in and around Kosong, as directed by spotter aircraft. Having returned fire and silenced Communist shore battery gunners who had commenced firing at her, on the twentieth, *Hamner* proceeded to rendezvous with the cruiser *Rochester* (CA-124) and steamed for Yokosuka. Mooring at berth number four in Yokosuka on the thirty-first, and after the supply officer returned to the ship with some $22,000 in MPC money, paying the crew their semimonthly monies, port and starboard liberty commenced.

During this time, the effectiveness of the naval blockade, and the enemy's failure to oppose it actively, opened both Korean coasts for the application of an effective bombardment and interdiction effort.

By the third of February, the destroyer had departed Yokosuka, and by midday was participating in ASW and Hunter-Killer exercises (firing depth charges and Hedgehogs) with the submarine USS *Blackfin* (SS-322), and *Sea Fox* (SS-402), in and around Atamia, Japan. On February 8, having completed ASW exercises, including numerous nights of ferrying her crew by motor whaleboat to the town, the destroyer steamed for Buckner Bay, Okinawa, where she conducted barrier patrol exercises for an additional week with the submarines.

Departing Buckner Bay on February 16, *Hamner* proceeded to the northern Taiwan Strait and commenced single ship patrol duty. During this time, she steamed in and out of Takao Harbor, Taiwan, where various units of the Pacific Fleet and Chinese Nationalist forces harbored.

Relieved from patrol duty on February 29, the destroyer steamed for Hong Kong where her crew enjoyed liberty before departing Victoria Harbor on March 4, en route for Sasebo, Japan, and duty off the east coast of Korea. Naval dispatches reaching *Hamner* during this time reported that an American destroyer had tracked a "skunk" by radar at a plotted speed as high as twenty-five knots. Concern among her crew was that Communist forces at last planned to oppose the strangling UN naval blockade with torpedo boats.

Proceeding back into hostile waters, *Hamner* on March 18 was once again firing at onshore targets directed by Shore Fire Control Parties (SFCPs) on the peninsula near Suwon Dan and Nan Do Island. On the morning of March 22 (0045), the destroyer was taken under fire by Communist shore installations with illumination and direct fire, estimated to be 105 mm projectiles. Zigzagging at thirty knots to avoid hits, *Hamner* counterfired using all five-inch and three-inch guns aboard, escaping all incoming rounds. Continuing H&I support throughout March, the destroyer on April 3 found herself screening two minesweepers off Kojo near Hill 64 when 7 star shells' airbursts at 2310 illuminated the skies and minesweepers. Closing the distance (at flank speed) between herself and the minesweepers, *Hamner* commenced counter-battery fire as five more airbursts fifty yards short in range of the minesweepers (three hundred yards astern of *Hamner*) came in. By 2355, the Communist guns became silent, and the destroyer continued her duty of screening the minesweepers as they swept the area. Having completed firing on two targets spotted by aircraft, the following day (April 4), *Hamner* again was maneuvering at flank speed counterfiring as she assisted ROK sampans taken under fire by shore batteries near Suwon Dan lighthouse.

The enemy had very few radar-controlled coastal guns, which meant that at nighttime, *Hamner* and her sister blockading ships could move closer ashore for their intercepting and gunnery efforts, with far less danger from enemy counter-batteries.

The eighth of April (1455) found the destroyer investigating two sampans which were identified friendly south of Nan Do. With all engines stopped, and a slight headway on the ship, one of the sampans drifted into the starboard side, amidships, damaging two stanchions at frame 115. The damage was considered minimal. Throughout the remainder of April and into May, *Hamner* conducted numerous H&I fire support mission in and around Kojo, Suwon Dan, and the Kosong area with the USS *Iowa* (BB-61), including the cruiser *Juneau* (CLAA-119) and carrier *Princeton* (CV-13).

Departing the bombline on May 12, the destroyer steamed for Yokosuka, where she unloaded ammunition, and on the fourteenth set sail for Midway, Hawaii, and the States, arriving in San Diego 31 May 1952, mooring at 0959 at Broadway Pier. A happy day for all hands!

Having undergone yard repairs, training, and gunnery exercises with an almost complete change of officers and enlisted personnel, *Hamner* on January 2, 1953 once again was underway for WestPac, anticipating heavy action in Korea.

Steaming to Hawaii where she participated in ASW exercises until January 19, the greyhound continued her westward journey, refueling at Midway Island whereupon she set sail for Sasebo, Japan.

Arriving at Sasebo on January 30, *Hamner*, by February 2, was again on the bombline conducting night H&I fire and shore bombardment while operating with the battleship *Missouri* (BB-63), cruiser *Los Angeles* (CA-135), and carrier *Valley Forge* (CVA-45) in and around Wonsan Harbor.

During this time, her night watch would try to catch a little sleep while the crew on duty continued patrolling the harbor, constantly on the lookout for enemy craft who might try to attack ships bombarding the harbor coast. To most of the *Hamner* destroyer's men, worse than either the blistering summer heat or the biting winter cold was the tedious routine of the war as the endless siege of Wonsan went on and on. The city itself was strategically located on Korea's east coast in the relatively tideless Sea of Japan, and was the principal seaport of North Korea. The harbor was large (three hundred square miles) and naturally protected from storms. In a part of the world often plagued with typhoons, the Japanese had named the port the "Harbor of Refuge" because it was rarely in any storm track.

By March 6, *Hamner* had been dispatched from TF-77 operations and was en route to Yokosuka via the Shimonoseki Strait, between the Japanese islands of Honshu and Kynshu, arriving on the seventh where her crew enjoyed liberty until it again departed for Korean waters on the eighteenth. Arriving off Kosong three days later, *Hamner* maneuvered into Wosan Harbor via passage between the mainland and the south side of Yodo Island, firing at bunkers emplacements and targets of opportunity. Breaking away from H&I on the twenty-fourth, the destroyer proceeded to investigate a twenty-foot sampan, containing nine men, two thousand yards offshore. Interrogation by a ROK Navy ensign attached to the *Hamner* for training purposes proved the craft and personnel to be South Koreans. At 0845 on the twenty-eighth, her crew spotted five stranded personnel on a rock three thousand yards from Suwon Dan. Sending her gun crew, CIC and the ship's control stations to General Quarters, *Hamner* commenced maneuvering on various courses and speed to investigate the personnel. By midmorning, a helicopter from the cruiser *Los Angeles* commenced transferring the personnel to *Hamner*. Preliminary interrogation of the Koreans disclosed they were apparently friendly civilian agents but were unable to produce positive identification. By midmorning end, *Hamner*'s motor whaleboat with an armed detail aboard had transferred the Koreans to the ROK Fifteenth Army Division at Mach-ajin-ni, a point fifteen miles south of Suwon Dan. Thereafter, she commenced independent shore bombardment of Mach-ajin-ni, supporting the ROK army division.

Back on the bombline as the siege of Wonsan Harbor continued, *Hamner* at 1325 on April 1 sighted a thirty-six-foot motor sampan at a distance of five miles (speed nine knots), showing an incomplete set of recognition signals. Upon stopping the sampan, interrogation personnel aboard disclosed the sampan to be friendly ROK fishermen. Returning to her patrol station on the Wonsan bombline, the destroyer, by the third, was again taken under attack off Yodo Island by shore batteries as approximately six rounds fell two hundred yards of her port beam including two airburst explosions (a near straddle at nine thousand yards, accurate fire by the Communist gunners).

Detached from the task force on the fifth of April, *Hamner* steamed for Yokosuka, where she moored on the sixth, alongside her sister ships in a nest. Here, an LCM while in the process of "landing" on the fantail did major damage to the stern depth charge rack of the *Chandler*, and major damage to the stern depth charge rack on *Hamner*.

April 17 found *Hamner* underway proceeding to ASW exercises in the area of Sagami, Japan. Upon completion, the destroyer anchored off Atami, and her crew, using the motor whaleboat, commenced brief shore liberty. Departing anchorage, *Hamner* steamed for Buckner Bay, Okinawa, and by May 1, was steaming in the Taiwan Strait, en route to BoKo K, Pescadores Island where it anchored. Having completed patrol duty in the northern waters of the strait during the first week of May, the destroyer steamed for Hong Kong for three days of crew rest and recreation, before departing for Sasebo and duty in Korean waters, arriving the twenty-second. By June 2, *Hamner* was off Nando Island where her whaleboat returned to the ship with an ROK soldier suffering from gunshot wounds. The next day, having transferred the soldier to the cruiser *St. Paul*, the destroyer returned to the bombline involving the siege of Wonsan conducting H&I and investigating unidentified crafts.

When in range of enemy guns, *Hamner* stayed "buttoned up," and personnel were forbidden to expose themselves topside. During the hot summer off Wonsan, temperatures below deck were stifling, and rest was impossible for many who found the irregular gunfire (constant jarring) too much for sleeping.

Hamner fired her last projectiles at North Korea forces at 1425 on July 26, 1953 off Point Silver (south of Wonsan), expending some 120 rounds of five-inch projectiles. At 1000 the following day (July 27), the crew was informed that an armistice agreement between the United Nations, the North Koreans, and Chinese Communist had been signed. The agreement provided for a cessation of hostilities at 2200 that day. At 2200, *Hamner* was conducting assigned patrols approximately nine miles for the North Korean coast, and in no case less than four miles from North Korean boundaries or island in accordance with the agreement. The crew was informed that cessation of hostility was then in effect between the subject parties, and future patrols would be on the "friendly line." The Communist gunners in Wonsan by that time were to succeed in neither of their missions of ever sinking the *Hamner* or her sister ships, nor could they drive the US Navy out of the harbor. The siege in Wonsan had lasted 861 days and ended as it had begun, with minesweepers sweeping and destroyers firing at targets until a minute before the 2200-hour deadline.

Steaming in the vicinity of latitude 38-39 degrees N, longitude 128-28.5 degrees E, on July 31, *Hamner* sighted a body in the water. She used her motor whaleboat to retrieve the body which once aboard was identified as a male, non-Caucasian, cause of death unknown. Personal effects found on the body were one US Army .45 caliber pistol, four gold rings, one wristwatch, one sheath knife, one US Army Corps of engineering pocket compass with the letters "K.I.A." scratched thereon, and an undetermined amount of Korean paper currency. The body was wrapped in canvas and placed on the fantail, later being transferred by motor whaleboat at Mach-ajin-in Point to the Fifteenth ROK Army Corps.[6]

Departing the "friendly line" on August 5, *Hamner* steamed for Yokosuka, where her supply officer left the ship with $46,944 in MPC to exchange for US currency. On the sixth, she was underway for the States, stopping at Midway, Pearl Harbor, and Long Beach, where on the twenty-first, she off-loaded ammunition. At 0900 on August 22, 1953, *Hamner* steamed into San Diego harbor, where it moored at the north side Navy Pier. It was a great and peaceful day for *Hamner's* crew.

---

[6] Between 1952 and 1953, two destroyer men lost their lives aboard the *Hamner*. On 21 May 1952, Richard M. Muberg (MMFN) was lost at sea off Midway Island as *Hamner* steamed for Hawaii. On 9 May 1953, Russel O. Triplett (TP3) died aboard after consuming bad alcohol ashore in Keelung, Taiwan.

Jason Freeze 1951-54

Lewis Turner 1951-54

Sampan

CHAPTER 5

—●—

Tin Can Sailor, 1953–1957

In November, 1953, the USS *Hamner* entered the US Naval Shipyard at Long Beach, California, for post Korean War modifications. With the crew stationed in barracks at the base, an array of extensive work began on improvement to the ship which included removing the entire steel 01 deckhouse and replacing it with aluminum in order to reduce topside weight. New SPS-6B air-search and SG-7 surface-search radar systems were installed. The main battery radar fire-control was upgraded by the installation of an Mk-25 system and an improved aircraft identify friend-or-foe (IFF) system was fitted aboard to support the Combat Information Center (CIC). New central radio room transmitting and receiving equipment was installed including a UHF 400Mhz transmitter. The electronic shop located next to the captain's quarter was relocated aft to the starboard side, adjoining the emergency transmitter room (abeam the second funnel on the main deck) which carried the ship's 500-watt radio transmitter. New S-11 sonar and an underwater telephone (AN/UQC-1) were installed including new ECM and SLR-2 equipment with their antennas mounted to the aft funnel and the yardarm ends. Part of the upgrade resulted in the removal of the depth charge projectors (K-guns alongside the after-deck house which had obstructed the sides of the deck for han-dling lines.) Long bench tables in the crew's mess deck were removed and replaced with new four-seat tables. Also, the installation of an all new operational dumbwaiter between the galley and mess deck was accomplished. Leaving the shipyard in January 1954, the USS *Hamner* (DD-718) was again ready for sea duty with Destroyer Division-111, Squadron 11 comprised of the USS *Wiltsie* (DD-716), *Chandler* (DD-717), and the *Chevalier* (DD-805).

Departing on her sixth WestPac tour in March 1954, and after a relaxing three-week stay in Hawaii, the ship proceeded to Yokosuka, Japan, where she moored alongside the supply ship USS *Hamul* (AK-25) before commencing sea operations in the Far East.

By early May, *Hamner* was on plane guard assignment and training operations in the Philippines, operating out of Subic Bay. During this period, she visited the port city of Manila for the first time where the sunken remains of many World War II naval vessels could be seen. By the end of May, *Hamner* found herself in harm's way as the United States assembled, in waters off French Indochina, the largest naval battle group since the end of World War II, threatening to strike Viet Minh forces if captive French prisoners taken during the fall of French Indochina were not treated by the accords reached in Geneva. *Hamner* stayed on station with the battle group until the crisis was defused.

Prowling the eastern coast of Japan on a balmy June evening, the word was "Lookout to bridge. Atami in sight."

"All stop. Let go the anchor. Liberty, liberty call. Away the motor whaleboat." And to the gambler sailors' delight, pachinko parlors were in sight.

By midyear, after months of operation in the Yokosuka area, which included anti-submarine exercises, *Hamner* returned south for patrol duty in Taiwan Strait.

With her whistle sounding the alarm as Red Chinese MiGs buzzed Kaohsiung Harbor, crewmen scrambled on the run from dock side beer halls, leaping aboard as *Hamner* headed for open water at "all ahead full," sinking a fishing boat in her wake. Waiting for Hamner's return dockside, Chinese officials demanded compensation. Afterward, this was the ship's squawk box message of the day:

> Now all hands, hear this. This is your captain speaking. I want each of you to never forget

that in the defense of Nationalist China, your government has just paid $800 to Chinese officials to compensate for the loss of one of their fishing boats.

Sasebo, Japan was visited on conclusion of duty in Taiwan, and after a short period in Korean waters, the ship sped on her long-awaited homeward journey to San Diego. On September 12, 1954, *Hamner* was home at last, whereupon she commenced preparation for her next WestPac tour.

Having undergone a three-month overhaul at the Long Beach Naval Shipyard and months of rugged training exercises, *Hamner* departed on June 28, 1955 with DesDiv-111 for WestPac cruise.

Sailing to Hawaii, where her crew spent a relaxing week, it proceeded to Midway Island, and by mid-July, arrived in Yokosuka.

"You are out of uniform, sailor. Call the master-at-arms (MA) to the quarterdeck," barked the officer of the deck in Yokosuka as a soldier (learning of *Hamner's* arrival) came up the gangway to visit his twin brother who was a sailor aboard. (Editor's note: Ken's twin brother, Keith, was in the Army at the same time Ken was serving in the navy. We think this was an unplanned visit from Keith.)

Notwithstanding the many crises in her day, a most frightening event occurred during night operations on September 23, 1955. While participating in a carrier task force operation in the South China Sea, the aircraft carrier USS *Boxer* (CVA-21) made a sudden, unexpected course change, placing itself on a direct collision course with the *Hamner*. As the *Boxer* was bearing down from a relative position forward of the port beam, Seaman Kent Madsen alerted the captain with these words: "Captain, is that carrier supposed to be there?" Captain Thompson took the con, and *Hamner* maneuvered hard right rudder first to starboard, then hard left rudder to port, fishtailing her stern away from the *Boxer* as she passed under the flare of the *Boxer's* hull. At almost the same time, the emergency collision whistle commenced, blowing four short distinctive blasts. With sailors running frantically in all directions on the main deck, some not recognizing the four-blast meaning like myself, I proceeded up a starboard side ladder for a life jacket located on the 01 deck. Reaching the 01 and looking nearly straight up before the fore and aft smoke funnels, I saw the *Boxer*, and watched as the forward lookout of the carrier dropped his earphones and ran off as *Hamner* passed less than five feet ahead of the *Boxer*. The *Boxer* command later indicated that with its flight deck some fifty-five feet above the waterline, and with the *Hamner*'s foremast at ninety feet as the destroyer leaned heavy as she turned, he did not know if the *Hamner* had been rammed as it passed beneath his view.

"Gawd, was I scared!" remarked one crewman.

By August, *Hamner* was again at sea involved with ASW and task force operations. In early September, she steamed into Hong Kong Harbor for a week of rest and relaxation before departing for Sasebo (Japan) and tender availability.

Tragedy struck the hearts of each crew member while in Sasebo Harbor, Japan, as the words *Man Overboard* were passed aboard the *Hamner*. Petty Officer Robert *Chevalier* of the USS *Chevalier* drowned while attempting to board a motor whaleboat that had brought him to *Hamner*.[7] Departing Sasebo, *Hamner* steamed south for the port cities of Keelung and Kaohsiung (Taiwan) for patrol duty. Little did the crew realize the rough water ride ahead. Reflecting back, sailors recall a more pleasant but rough ride stateside.

"All aboard!" the operator had shouted as *Hamner* sailors with ladies on arm joyfully boarded the Cyclone Roller Coaster at the Long Beach Amusement Park. Picket patrol in the typhoon rough waters in the Taiwan Strait was not so joyful. A roller coaster ride at its best tested every sailor at his best.

"Admiral, sir. We just took a forty-five-degree roll. We need to change course. The seas can only be described as mountainous" was the captain's radio message, as *Hamner* rode the *camel's back* waves for twenty days.

---

[7] Petty Officer Robert Chevalier of the USS *Chevalier* (DD-805), was the grandson of the Chevalier's namesake, drowned while attempting to board a motor whaleboat that had brought him to *Hamner*.

Returning in early November 1955 to Yokosuka, she tied alongside the destroyer tender USS *Frontier* (AD-25) for two weeks, before sailing to Kobe for five days of liberty in one of the most scenic regions of Japan. Leaving Kobe, *Hamner* put into Yokosuka before departing for the States.

Splash, splash. "What is that splashing?" the officer of the deck asked the seaman of the watch in Yokosuka Harbor, at 0300.

"Permission to come aboard, sir?" asked the sailor, with his shoes in one hand and his white "dixie cup" in the other, as he climbed the gangway. "I missed the last motor whaleboat and was afraid *Hamner* would sail off for the States leaving me behind."

"Permission granted, sailor."

"Land ahoy, sailors" was the lookout's call on December 15, 1955 as Point Loma beckoned on the horizon. Docking at the Broadway Pier, with her band playing and her crew in dress uniform lining the deck, it was "home at last, home at last," in time for a joyful Christmas.

Departing San Diego on July 13, 1956, *Hamner* set sail on her eighth WestPac cruise. Steaming to Hawaii, then toward the coral atoll of Kwajalein (Marshall Islands) where it refueled, *Hamner* continued her journey southward, crossing the equator on July 28. On that day, Neptunus Rex and his gang boarded *Hamner*, and some 211 pollywogs from a crew complement of 234 became shellback-strong. On August 2, with kangaroos watching and sailors gawking, DesDiv-111 arrived "down under" at Brisbane, Australia, the first United States naval vessels to visit the city since the end of WWII in 1945.

With an Australian army band playing, *Hamner* bid farewell to Brisbane on August 7 and sailed northward, crossing the equator again as she headed for Guam (Marianas Islands). Leaving Guam, she proceeded to Yokosuka for Task Force 77 hunter-killer operations with submarines and the carrier USS *Boxer* (CVA-21).

By the twenty-fourth of October, having visited the port of Kobe, along with the carrier USS *Essex* (CV-9), *Hamner* passed through the famous San Bernardino Straits on her way to the Philippines for dry dock repairs. Upon leaving the Philippines, she returned to Sasebo and Seventh Fleet operations.

In early February 1957, *Hamner* bid sayonara to Japan, setting a course eastward for the States. Returning on February 19, 1957 to her home port, San Diego, she commenced crew training and preparation for her next WestPac cruise.

718
USS Hamner

Raymond Beck 1954-57
(Kangaroo is wearing Ray's cover)

Ken Ericksen 1953-56

Keith Hipwell 1955

Joseph Keadle 1951-55

USS Boxer (CV-21) with TF 77

The *Boxer* and *Hamner* almost collided on 9/3/55

Tom Proctor 1951-55

Duane Rose 1952-54

Zeke Sicotte 1953-55

Jimmy Tighe 1952-55

CHAPTER 6

Underway—Shift Color, 1957–1958

Life was never so good. Beer was fifteen cents a mug, a bunk on Saturday night at the San Diego Army Navy YMCA was "one buck," girls on the beach were plentiful, and navy was the best in town.

I believe destroyer duty aboard the *Hamner* was the best navy billet in its time. The smell of "good chow" from the galley was always in the air, and evening movies on the fantail were a sailor's treat at the end of a long day's work.

At sea, CIC buzzed with action during AWS exercises.

"'Gatekeeper, gatekeeper' (*Chevalier*), this is 'Fish Market' (*Hamner*). You are sister, I am brother, I am hot, I will smother. Inform 'Hay Marker' (DesDivison-111)."

Weekend liberty was never to be missed. If in dense fog, *Hamner* would find San Diego port with radar, then using beam-to-beam sonar, locate the mooring buoy. Piping of the boatswain's whistle told it all. "Liberty call, liberty call, away the motor whaleboat." A happy crew was always waiting.

From battlewagon row, lights from the El-Cortez "Sky Room" told a sailor where a gentleman should be, and the United Water Taxi Company taxis prowled the fleet moored at bay. Broadway Avenue twinkled with penny arcades, and the Seven Seas Locker Club was a home away from home for Tin Can sailors. On Saturday nights, white hats bobbed as far as an eye could see, and the "Pink Palace" (Naval Medical Center San Diego) was there for the fleet to see.

Departing San Diego on August 2, 1957, in company with the heavy cruiser *Los Angeles* (CA-135) and seven ships of DesRon-11 to attend the Seattle Seafair, *Hamner* set a course northward and sailed along the Pacific coast toward the Straits of Juan de Fuca and Seattle, Washington. Participating in gunnery exercises off Astoria, Oregon, *Hamner* fired twelve salvos at one of two targets (LSIs) with one possible hit. Distancing herself from the target, *Hamner* observed as the cruiser with ships of DesDiv-112 sank the two LSI(L)'s. Mooring at Pier 91 in Seattle on August 6, *Hamner*'s crew experienced five days of liberty during the fair before departing on her return trip to San Diego. *Hamner* arrived at her home port on the fourteenth of August, whereby she continued preparations for her upcoming WestPac tour.

In preparation for getting underway to the Far East in September, *Hamner* experienced an unexplained rapid depletion of fresh water. The basic issue was that although enough water was being distilled, huge amounts of boiler feed water were being lost somewhere in the closed circuit between the condenser, the feed pumps, and the boilers. Unable to find any leaks, and faced with the fact that it was the last night in the States with no resolution to the problem, eleven thousand gallons of feed water had to be transferred to the destroyer via the graces of the USS *Hector* (AR-6). *Hamner* was now ready to set underway.

On September 16, 1957, DesDiv-111, comprised of the USS *Wiltsie* (DD-716), *Chandler* (DD-717), *Chevalier* (DD-805), and the *Hamner* (DD-718), departed San Diego for WestPac and joined up with the carrier USS *Ticonderoga* (CVA-14) for air operation while the carrier was en route to Hawaii. Bypassing Hawaii, the Destroyer Division took on replenishments at sea from the USS *Hassayampa* (AO-145), including a full load of water for the *Hamner*, and set a fifteen-knot speed of advance (SOA) heading 2,900 miles southward for Suva (Fiji Islands), a British colony at the time, to attend, by governor's invitation, the Hibiscus Festival. On September 24, *Hamner* crossed the equator and Davy Jones, royal scribe to Neptunus Rex, was back aboard with a message from the Raging Main.

"Where are those slimy pollywogs?"

Again, *Hamner's* crew faced the ordeal of becoming shell-back-strong. Nearing Suva on the twenty-eighth, *Hamner* found herself standing by with lines in hand ready to assist her sister ship because *Chevalier* had run precariously low on fuel.

Departing Suva and steaming southward for Melbourne, *Hamner* took the opportunity to conduct a target acquisition exercise with Australian Spitfire fighter aircraft prior to her arrival on the sixth of October. Thoroughly enjoying a week's stay in Melbourne (where she took on five thousand gallons of water from the *Chevalier*), *Hamner* again set out to sea, arriving next at Manus, Admiralty Islands, after conducting live torpedo practice while en route. Continuing northward to Guam, where she paused for liberty and replenishment, before setting a northwest course, eventually arriving in Yokosuka on October 27, 1957. While there, the USS *Dixie* (AD-14) lent assistance in treating the water consumption problem. No one was ever quite sure just what solved the problem, or whether it even was solved, but before setting sail again, *Hamner* had water, and water hours were no longer in effect.

On November 11, 1957, *Hamner* was again underway on gunnery and sea operations, arriving the latter part of the month at Buckner Bay (Okinawa), where she took on replenishments before heading to sea for "Operation Strongback." After participating with the carrier USS *Princeton* (CVS-37) and DesDiv-253 in convoy barrier screening ASW and hunter-killer exercises through November 27, *Hamner*, and the rest of the convoy, proceeded to Subic Bay.

By December 9, the Destroyer Division was once again underway operating with the carrier *Ticonderoga* (CVA-14), the cruiser USS *Los Angeles* (CA-135) and USS *Roanoke* (CL-145). *Hamner's* provisions were supplied by highline from the USS *Grafffias* (AF-29), and ammunition from the USS *Mauna Kea* (AE-22). Fuel needs were met by the USS *Taluga* (AO-62). By the middle of December, *Hamner* was back in Yokosuka where she enjoyed Christmas and New Year's before putting but to sea.

Underway January 1, 1958, *Hamner's* next port of call was Hong Kong, where she stayed until the fourteenth before commencing operations out of Kaohsiung (Taiwan) which included combined gunnery operations with five Chinese Nationalist patrol boats in the Taiwan Strait.

At first light on February 11, *Hamner* slipped past the dark silhouette of Corregidor and moored alongside the USS *Bryce Canyon* (AD-36) in Manila Bay, commencing nine days of tender availability. She then departed for Subic Bay and on to Okinawa. By the twenty-seventh, she was back in the Philippines at Dingalan Bay (Luzon).

Back at sea on a combined United States and Philippines Navy Amphibious exercise (Operation Strongback), from February 23 through March 3, *Hamner* participated in convoy tactics while escorting the amphibious movement group from Okinawa to Dingalan Bay. There she participated in convoy tactics by blockading the submarine USS *Bluegill* (SSK-282) from the defenseless ships landing the "invasion" force on the beach.

Leaving Dingalan Bay, the destroyer proceeded to Guam (Marianas Islands), where for three days, commencing March 7, she participated in aircraft target acquisition involving aircraft from the island. Leaving the Marianas, the Destroyer Division set a northeasterly course toward Midway Island, then on to Hawaii and the States. By March 23, 1958, she was home at last, home at last in San Diego.

Maneuvering off San Diego in May 1958, the Destroyer Division was ordered to sink a surplus, expendable LST. At a range of two thousand yards, each ship was authorized to expend in turn one live MK-16 (twenty-one-inch torpedo). *Hamner*'s turn was last. All of her sister ships had fired and missed the target. Firing her torpedo, she commenced to broach, although dead on target, it passed beneath the LST. With all gun batteries blazing, the division sank the LST.

In July 1958, *Hamner* along with the USS *Wiltsie* (DD-716) and the USS *Bennington* (CVA-20) steamed north to Canada to attend British Columbias Centennial and to participate in the International Naval Review. On July 15, Princess Margaret of the United Kingdom reviewed the combined fleet from the review ship HMCS *Crescent*, and shortly afterward, *Hamner* departed for San Diego, visiting the Port of Everett, Washington, on her return trip.

By the end of the decade, *Hamner*'s home port, San Diego, was changing. The Pacific Square Ballroom and Paris Inn (favorite night-spots for Tin Can sailors) had closed. Big band music was fading away, rock and roll was coming of age, and bikinis were in at Mission Beach. Lane Field, the Tower Theater, and Pullman's Cafeteria were also gone. A sailor could still buy a cup of coffee for ten cents at Bernie's Café at the foot of Broadway Avenue before boarding an LVP at Navy Landing to ships moored in San Diego Bay.

When not deployed in the Pacific, *Hamner* and her crew trained out of San Diego, California.

Del Mancuso 1956-58

John Peede 1956-57

Crew preparing torpedo mount

torpedo ready
to fire

In flight on target!

Torpedo mount back in
underway position

CHAPTER 7

Prowling the Pacific Ocean, 1958–1961

Tied alongside of the USS *Dixie* (AD-14), proudly wearing her thirteenth battle efficiency "E," *Hamner* prepared to commence her tenth WestPac cruise on November 22, 1958. She would be joined with the rest of the destroyers in DesDiv-111: USS *Wiltsie* (DD-716), *Chandler* (DD717), and *Chevalier* (DD-805).

Steaming to Hawaii, then onto Midway Island (pausing briefly at each island), *Hamner* continued her westward journey, and on December 10, steamed into Yokosuka, Japan (after dodging typhoon Olga), moored next to the USS *Piedmont* (AD-17).

Having celebrated Christmas Day with a party at the chief petty officers (CPO) club in Yokosuka, *Hamner* was once again underway on December 26, heading for Kaoshiung, Taiwan, teeming with Chinese Nationalist troops and uncounted slit-skirted ladies, arriving at the port city on the last day of 1958, where her crew celebrated New Year's Eve.

Reminding Asia of American determination and strength in the struggle against Communists, the destroyer engaged in exercises with the Taiwan Patrol Force throughout the first half of January 1959, shortly after a flare-up of the Quemoy-Matsu crisis had occurred.

By late January, *Hamner* steamed into the *Pearl of the Orient* (Hong Kong Harbor), where she stayed for five days as her crew thoroughly enjoyed rest and relaxation. At Tiger Balm Garden, a sailor asked, "Where are the tigers?" as Hong Kong tour guides looked on with a smile. Departing Hong Kong at month end, *Hamner's* next stop was Subic Bay (Philippines), where she entered dry dock for badly needed repairs.

Setting a course northward on February 14, *Hamner* rendezvoused with the new United States aircraft carrier USS *Ranger* (CV-67) for sea operation. Operating out of Japan and Okinawa with the carrier for the next two months, she spent long hours in position as a plane guard rescue destroyer. Occasionally, an oiler would come alongside to supply necessary fuel, requiring fuel stations to be manned and highlines detail set "as part of work involving sea operations." *Hamner* belonged out there, doing a destroyer's job and doing it well.

By late March, *Hamner* was back in Yokosuka where she made preparations for her next stop, Guam, Marianas Islands, arriving there early in April 1959. The one-week stop was mostly work and more work for the crew, but a few crew members were able to do some sightseeing, visiting Gab Gab beach.

Leaving Guam, *Hamner* set a course southward for Melbourne, Australia. Nearing the equator on April 22, 1959, Neptunus Rex, with his goon squad (an unruly lot), was back aboard with subpoenas and summons, searching for slimy pollywogs. By day's end, Neptunus Rex and his gang sank into the sea, and *Hamner's* crew was again shellback-strong.

Arriving in late May at Melbourne for the "Coral Sea Festival" (which was named after the pivotal WWII carrier battle which set the stage for the Battle of Midway in 1942), all hands aboard *Hamner* thoroughly enjoyed the celebration. Winding her way back down from the Yarra River and into Prince Phillip Bay at festival's end, *Hamner* headed for the open sea where she set a northward course to Suva (Fiji Islands), and was greeted on the pier by a native band and onlookers. After a short stay, *Hamner* continued her northbound eastern journey toward Pearl Harbor and the States. On May 19, 1959, it was home at last, home at last as she docked at Pier 1, San Diego, California.

One month later, *Hamner* entered the Long Beach Naval Shipyard for overhaul and preparations for her next WestPac cruise.

The scuttlebutt was "the WestPac would be before the end of the year," as *Hamner* sailors worked away the last days of 1959. By January 19, 1960, *Hamner* was underway on the WestPac cruise, with her sister ships of DesDiv-111.

Sailing to far-off ports, *Hamner* sailors saw a world they had never known, and one they would never forget. After spending nearly two months involved in carrier task force operations in the vicinity of Japan, *Hamner* sailed for Hong Kong.

"Welcome to Hong Kong Uss *Hamner* Dd-718" was the banner of the day as the cleanup gang of Mary Soo and her girls with paintbrushes in hand greeted *Hamner* on her stay. With shoe cobblers, tailors, photographers, and trinket shops spawning about her deck, sailors of the *Hamner* always had a great stay. At the scullery, Mary Soo was there to sort food on the sailors' tray to help feed hungry Chinese refugees from mainland China.

By April 1960, *Hamner* was underway with the USS *Morton* (DD-948), escorting the USS *Bonhomme Richard* CVA-19) to Bombay, India. On her return trip, the task group crossed the equator in the Indian Ocean, and visited Singapore. Both ports were first time visits for *Hamner*.

"Captain! We have a problem, sir. Rex and his gang are aboard and they want to talk to you."

"You are in my territorial water (latitude zero degrees)," raged the royal scribe of Imperial Neptunus Rex. I thought I had made a clean sweep of those slimly pollywogs aboard this vessel in the 1950s!"

"Now hear this, now hear this. This is the captain speaking. All pollywogs muster on the main deck on the double for conversion to shellbacks."

And again, *Hamner*'s crew became shellback-strong.

Returning from WestPac with Destroyer Division-111 on May 31, 1960, she spent the remainder of the year in training and local exercises off San Diego and the Channel Islands.

"Captain, torpedo off and running, sir!"

"Aye, aye, commence firing" were the words of the day as *Hamner* participated with sister ships of DesDiv-111 in the sinking of the *Belle Isle* (AKS-21).[8]

In the black of the night, the bridge plan position indicator (PPI) scope always told a sailor where he should be.

"Engine room, bridge."

"Engine room, aye."

"Slow to one-third."

"Aye, aye."

"Helmsman, steer three degrees to port and hold her steady," was the word of the wheelhouse as the night slowly passed.

By April 1961, all preparations were completed, and *Hamner* was once again underway with DesDiv-111 less the USS *Wiltsie* (DD-716) for her twelfth WestPac cruise.

While en route, *Hamner* stopped at Pearl Harbor and Midway Island. She then paused for voyage repairs at Guam. During the transit between Guam and Kaohsiung, Taiwan, the destroyer division was diverted to Subic Bay for additional backup of the Seventh Fleet's South China Sea forces. *Hamner*'s participation included carrier operations with the USS *Coral Sea* (CVA-43).

After the tension subsided in Laos, she proceeded to Kaohsiung, arriving on May 12, 1961, and thereafter assumed patrol duty in Taiwan Strait.

Upon being relieved of patrol duty on June 12, DesDiv-111 set course for Yokosuka, Japan, for tender availability and further assignments to Task group 77.5, including plane guard operations with the USS *Midway* (CVA-41).

On June 30, the division departed Yokosuka to join the USS *Midway* for close support of extensive carrier operations. DesDiv-111 was redesignated DesDiv-52 on July 1, 1961.

Near the end of July, Task Group 77.5, to which *Hamner* had been assigned as escort, stopped at Sasebo, Japan, for a rest and recreation visit. The visit was suddenly interrupted on July 30, 1961 by

---

8 *Belle Isle* was stricken from the Navy list in April 1960 and was sunk as a target later that year.

typhoons Helen and Ida, which were heading straight for Sasebo. Almost all naval units on the harbor, including Task Group 77.5 lost no time in getting underway and successfully evaded the typhoons, returning to Sasebo on August 2, 1961.

Subsequently, Task Group 77.5 engaged in operations including anti-submarine and anti-air warfare exercises, and on August 10, the task group steamed into Yokosuka Harbor. The highlights of the deployment for DesDiv-52 was a four-day ASW and communication exercise with units of Japan's navy called the Japanese Maritime Self-Defense Force.

On September 7, 1961, *Hamner* bid sayonara to Yokosuka for this cruise and steamed to Hong Kong for a short recreational visit before returning to the States. This visit was also interrupted by a tropical storm, and DesDiv-52 (less the *Chevalier*) were immediately underway for sea on September 9, 1961 and returned to Hong Kong the next day.

On September 12, 1961, the *Hamner*, along with the sister ships of DesDiv-52, sailed from Hong Kong with the USS *Midway* (CVA-41), USS *Topeka* (CLG-8), USS *McCain* (DL-3), and the USS *Prebke* (DLG-15). The division came home to San Diego on September 28, 1961.

Camp Hanford 1959

Destroyer Squadron 11 (DesRon 11)

USS Hamner wins another Battle Efficiency E

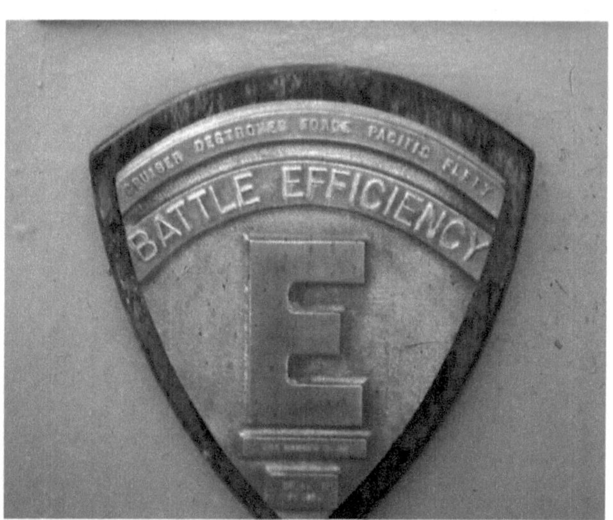

1959 Forward Gun Mounts

USS Morton (DD-948), USS Wiltsie (DD-716), USS
Hamner (DD-718), and USS DeHaven (DD-727)

CHAPTER 8

Commence Firing, 1962–1966

In January 1962, *Hamner* began a yearlong special overhaul in San Francisco known as a Fleet Rehabilitation and modernization (FRAM) with an emphasis on ASW improvements. While her crew lived in the barracks at Hunter's Point, she was fitted with a totally new superstructure and the United States navy's newest and most efficient armaments and equipment.

Machinery and electrical systems were updated and her gun armament was reduced from six to four five-inch guns. Mount 52 was removed (aft mount 53 was redesignated 52), including the removal of all three-inch 50 mm armament. New ASW armament fitted aboard consisted of RUR-5A ASROC ASE system carrying homing torpedoes or nuclear warheads (1x8, seventeen missiles) with launcher, control room, and magazine located between the ship's twin funnels, two 6-12.75 triple ASW (MK-32) homing torpedo tubes, located port and starboard forward to the bridge, as well as long-range SQS-23 hull sonar and an SPS-40 radar system. Also, facilities were provided for two revolutionary OH-50 pilotless Drone Anti-Submarine Helicopters (DASH), each scheduled to be placed aboard in 1964 and each designed to carry homing torpedoes. The original anti-ship torpedoes carried amid ships were displaced by the ASROC armaments. The new superstructure was aluminum, and the bridge was drastically enlarged and enclosed, with wings on each side. The introduction of drone helicopters on board required the addition of a flight deck aft as well as a large aircraft hangar to house the birds assigned. The new flight deck could be used for vertical underway replenishment, mail delivery, or personnel transfer, all by helicopter.

Upon completion of the FRAM conversion, her endurance distance was 5,800 miles at fifteen knots, fuel capacity was 650 tons, full load displacement was 3,533 tons, total shaft horsepower was 60,000 and her crew allowance was 14 officers and 260 enlisted men.

Hamner left the shipyard on December 5, 1962 and, after training, was once again underway on May 18, 1963 on another WestPac cruise. During this cruise in September, she became part of the amphibious ready group (ARG) in South Vietnam coastal waters. By year's end, *Hamner* was reassigned to DesDiv-72, DesRon 7, along with the USS *Wiltsie* (DD-716), USS *Chevalier* (DD-805) and USS *Roger* (DD-876).

On November 24, 1963, *Hamner* returned to San Diego where her crew enjoyed Thanksgiving Day. She then operated along the West Coast throughout 1964, knowing that on August 5, the first naval air strike against North Vietnam had commenced. During this same time period, DASH was placed on board.

Operations off the West Coast, including a regular overhaul at Hunter's Point Shipyard in South San Francisco, occupied *Hamner* for a good part of the remaining months in 1964. By late December 1964 (about the same time Navy River Patrol Force "Operation Game Warden" was activated in Vietnam), *Hamner* left the yard and steamed for San Diego. The plan was to be home for Christmas. However, while outside the Golden Gate during a gale in the middle of the night, *Hamner* lost the spring bearing on one of her shafts, necessitating an immediate return to the shipyard for further repairs. With wives and girlfriends waiting, many of her crew went to San Diego by bus for Christmas.

On January 5, 1965, *Hamner* departed San Diego on her second WestPac cruise since her FRAM. During the developing Vietnam crisis, during which the U.S. sought to protect South Vietnam from Communist oppression, Subic Bay (Philippines) became the most important forward base for the Seventh Fleet as it was close to the Gulf of Tonkin, and in 1965, *Hamner* spent most of her time in and out of this port. Arriving in Subic Bay on the twenty-seventh of January, *Hamner* escorted USS *Hancock* (CVA-19) to the Gulf of Tonkin for flight operations. This was only the *Hamner's* second cruise into Vietnamese waters (the first had been in May 1954). On March 15, 1965, she joined with the aircraft carrier *Coral Sea* (CVA-43) in "Yankee Team" operation, and on the tenth of May, *Hamner* headed north at flank speed to cover the US Seabee landing at Chu Lai. "Market Time" operations (coastal patrol against North Vietnam infiltration of South Vietnam) began five days later, and on May 20, 1965, a historical first occurred when *Hamner* became the first US Navy ship to bombard Communist forces located on the shores of South Vietnam. This was the first use of naval gunfire against hostile land targets since the Korean conflict. After becoming a part of history, *Hamner* screened Coral Sea (CVA-43), and then took part in the bombarding of Trung Phan on June 25. On July 1, 1965, *Hamner* covered the marines landing, from the USS *Iwo Jima* (LPH-2), at Quin Nhon.

As mid-July approached, the destroyer steamed for Hong Kong, and after a two-day stay, was chased out by typhoon Freda. *Hamner* then set sail for the port of Yokosuka, where her crew accomplished some last minute shopping before her departure on July 26 for the States. By early August, she reached San Francisco, and after a brief stay, departed for her home port. Memories of WestPac were soon dispelled when Pier 4 of the Naval Destroyer Base came into view, as she returned to San Diego.

During the first half of 1966, *Hamner* completed numerous stateside gunnery exercises, including naval gunfire support training in preparation for deployment. Her crew was excellent in handling the ship's gun batteries, resulting in no other ship being able to out-shoot her. One of these exercises involved towing the EX-*Lewis* (DE-535) out of San Diego Harbor to waters off San Clemente Island and sinking the former destroyer escort on April 21, 1966. A frightening moment occurred during an exercise when one round was accidently fired dead astern from mount 52.[9] Luckily, no ships were behind *Hamner* at the time.

On July 2, 1966, *Hamner* was underway again on her next WestPac Far East cruise. Her destination was "sunny tropical" Vietnam. The course west passed Hawaii, Midway Island, Guam, and onto Subic Bay. A slight course change was made due to a typhoon, resulting in *Hamner* entering the Philippines via the San Bernardino Straits. Experiencing unbearable heat and water hours (rationed water) as earlier crews had in the past, many crew members simply showered on deck during the tropical rainstorms.

By late July, *Hamner* was off the coastal waters of Vietnam, hammering away at enemy targets. Thereafter, following patrol duty, she steamed up Song Sai Gon (Saigon) River and engaged in harassment and interdiction shelling of Communist positions in the Rung Sat special zone. While there, the *Hamner* was called to guard the merchant marine vessel *Baton Rouge Victory* (Yard Number 2499) which had been mined in the river, until help arrived.

Assigned as part of Operation "Sea Dragon," the naval bombardment of the North Vietnamese coast, *Hamner* proceeded to Da Nang, where at night, her heavily armed motor whaleboat picked up several South Vietnamese liaison officers at a naval compound known as White Elephant, and the crews received a briefing on their new assignment. Taking aboard sixty civilian irregular defense troops (Cambodian mercenaries led by the navy), *Hamner* proceeded to transport them to a landing site where, in the early hours of the morning, she laid down preinvasion fire and sent them off in their boats to attack various village strongholds. During this mission, *Hamner* sank numerous enemy logistic craft.

Hamner did not always remain on the battle line. Steaming to Hong Kong, she was, as in the past, greeted by Mary Soo and her girls in their sampans. Captain to officer of the deck:

"Call away the motor whaleboat. I plan to go ashore at 0700."

---

[9] While operating off Vietnam in 1966, one crew member was accidentally killed in mount 52 during gunnery operations.

"Captain! Sir, that is not possible. We "lost" our motor whaleboat during the night! The Chinese have it for cleaning!" Luckily, it was returned (as planned) later that morning. Liberty for the *Hamner's* crew during the Vietnam War may have been at its best in Hong Kong.

Departing Hong Kong, *Hamner* proceeded to Subic Bay for upkeep, maintenance, and replenishment of stores, which allowed her crew time for some rest, relaxation, and beer drinking at Olongapo's "finest" beer palace (located at the east end of town).

Proceeding back into hostile waters off Vietnam and plane guard operations, *Hamner* soon rescued a downed pilot at night after a midair collision.

On October 1, 1966, *Hamner* joined Task Group 77.6 as plane guard for the USS *Oriskany* (CVA-34). While on this duty, she received an emergency call on October 26 from the carrier at 0700. "We have fire aboard." Speeding alongside, *Hamner* was the first ship to render assistance to the stricken carrier, in which forty-three men were killed, and over one hundred injured. For hours, *Hamner* sprayed water on the *Oriskany's* charred and buckled bulkheads. After the fight to save the carrier from sinking had been won, *Hamner* escorted it to Subic Bay for repairs.

After replenishing in Subic Bay, *Hamner* departed for the coast of North Vietnam, and in November, spent two weeks in operation "Traffic Cop," shelling and sinking Communist junks which had been bringing supplies to the Viet Cong in South Vietnam. On November 19, while detached with the USS *John R. Craig* (DD-858) near Vinh (North Vietnam), *Hamner* was taken under fire by Communist shore batteries. Although incoming rounds sprayed both destroyers with shrapnel, neither ship was damaged. On each occasion of enemy shelling, the American ships commenced counter-battery fire and maneuvered outside the range of their guns. Leaving the fighting zone on November 20, 1966, *Hamner* set course for the States.

Steaming first to Kaoshiung, Taiwan, where her crew enjoyed liberty and beer at Nancy's Harbor, she proceeded to get underway for Japan. Steaming toward Nagasaki, on the second leg of her long homeward-bound trip, it became necessary for *Hamner* to change course and head for Okinawa due to typhoon conditions. Arriving during the night at White Beach, some of her crew went on liberty while others stayed aboard to put a new coat of paint on the ship in preparation for the Nagasaki visit.

Having never visited the port of Nagasaki before, *Hamner*'s crew looked forward to a long liberty stay.

"Hey, Chief. What do you suppose that Japanese lady translator at pier end is trying to tell us?"

"Engine room, bridge"

"Engine room, aye,"

"EMERGENCY BACK" was the order from the officer of the deck as a loud crashing sound was heard.

"Aye, aye, bridge."

"I think she was trying to tell us to back the ship out." Looking at the seven-foot missing section in *Hamner*'s bow, the officer of the deck said to the seaman of the deck,

"I owe you a case of beer. I just ruined your new paint job." With emergency pumps operating, *Hamner* steamed to Yokosuka, where in dry dock, her famous "Nagasaki Notch" (including the 1952 Pearl Harbor dimple) was removed and a new bow section was placed on the ship.

A month and a day later, after leaving Vietnam, *Hamner* reached San Diego, where at year's end, she began preparations to meet her next challenge.

718
USS Hamner   1965

Jon Newcomer 1961-65

Daryl Patrick 1965-67

1963 – Far Left: G. Vienna, Ctr: R. DiPiazza, Far Right: J. Everett

Passing Point Loma in April 1963

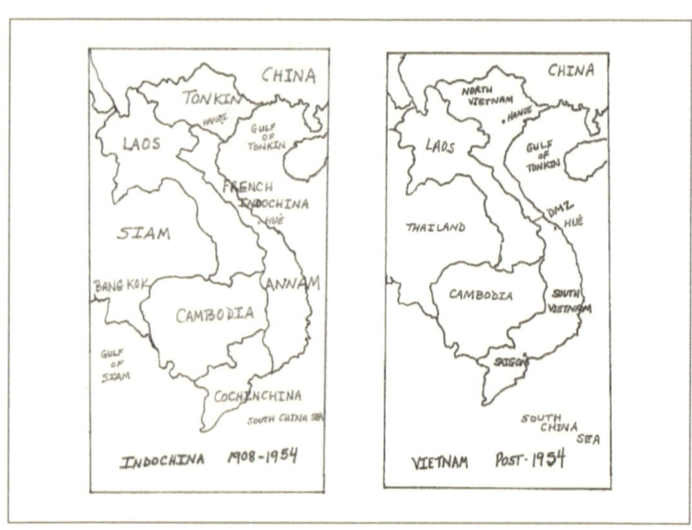

Lee Parsons 1965-67

Arnold Case 1961-64

1966 – ASROC crew: Kurth (Far Left), Sellers (Back), Edington (R-Fwd), Coldwater (Far right)

CHAPTER 9

Man Your Battle Stations, 1967–1968

After returning from the WestPac cruise in December 1966, the *Hamner* completed six months of training exercises out of her home port, San Diego. She departed on June 8, 1967 for the Pacific Northwest to participate in the annual Rose Festival at Portland, Oregon. During her five-day stay, thousands of visitors were guided through the destroyer before she returned to San Diego to continue training exercises in anticipation of her next WestPac cruise.

On September 19, 1967, *Hamner* got underway for WestPac, anticipating heavy action off Vietnam. After taking on fuel at Pearl Harbor, *Hamner* proceeded west via Midway Island, stopping two days at Yokosuka, Japan. She then proceeded to Okinawa for refueling, and by October 13, arrived in Subic Bay to take on replenishments. By October 20, 1967, *Hamner* was in the Tonkin Gulf on Yankee Station with the USS *Coral Sea* (CVA-43). During this period, *Hamner* supported in numerous flight operations, and conducted two search and rescues for downed aircraft. Requiring maintenance, *Hamner*'s next stop was Subic Bay where she spent six days before leaving for Hong Kong. After five rough days at sea, *Hamner* steamed into Hong Kong Harbor and commenced three days of rest and relaxation. Steaming from Hong Kong to Vietnam, naval gunfire support was the next assignment on *Hamner*'s schedule, and on

November 11, she proceeded to the lower III Corps area of South Vietnam to begin this activity.

Arriving on station November 13, 1967, *Hamner* relieved the destroyer USS (DD-759) thirty miles north of St. Jacques and expended 202 rounds of ammunition in support of troops ashore. The next two days found *Hamner* anchored at the mouth of the Long Tao river, where on the fourteenth, she fired 321 rounds of ammunition at various targets with good coverage. On the fifteenth, '79 rounds were fired, resulting in numerous bunkers and one sampan being damaged. Leaving the area, *Hamner* next rendezvoused for fuel from the USS *Chemung* (AO-30), and the following day was rearmed at sea by the USS *Mount Baker* (AE-4), taking aboard 600 rounds of 5"/38 inches ammunition.

On November 17, *Hamner* commenced shore bombardment fifty miles north of St. Jacques, expending fifty rounds, and the next day a few miles further south, expending one hundred rounds. Leaving the area, she was again rearmed by the Mount Baker, taking aboard five hundred rounds.

Arriving in Song Nga Bay on the nineteenth for harassment and interdiction firing, she expended ninety-one rounds. The next day, *Hamner* was back off St. Jacques where she expended fifty-one rounds in bombardment before taking on thirteen tons of groceries replenishment at sea from the USS *Graffias* (AF-29).

The following two days found *Hamner* continuing bombardment off St. Jacques, firing a total of 119 rounds. At 1200 on November 22, she was rearmed by USS *Mount Baker* (AE-4), taking aboard five hundred rounds, and by midafternoon, was back, station firing some eighty-one rounds by day's end.

On Thanksgiving Day, November 23, 1967, after expending 1,269 rounds during two weeks of NGFS, the destroyer was relieved on station by the USS *Perkins* (DD-877). The next day, having been refueled by the oiler USS *Cacapon* (AO-52), and in need of maintenance, *Hamner* proceeded to Sasebo, Japan, for a ten-day stay.

Arriving on November 29, a cold day in Sasebo, and having set about accomplishing necessary repairs, liberty was granted, to the delight of the crew. Tours were conducted to Nagasaki and to the resort town of Unzen, which her crew thoroughly enjoyed.

With snow falling, *Hamner* departed Sasebo on December 2 and headed for Vietnam, stopping on the way for overnight evaporator repairs at Kaohsiung, Taiwan.

By December 13, 1967, *Hamner* was again underway for sea as she readied herself for her next assignment Operation Sea Dragon. During *Hamner's* period on Operation Sea Dragon, which was in company with Her Majesty's Australian ship *Perth* (D-38), many hours were spent at General Quarters as the ship rode shotgun for the *Perth* and engaged in NGFS, often steaming within close range of North Vietnamese shore batteries.

On December 21, fifty-four crewmen were helicopter lifted to the USS *Ranger* (CVA-61) for the Bob Hope show which they really enjoyed.

Christmas day found *Hamner* participating in the very early morning (man overboard was called at 0130) search and successful rescue of a drowning sailor from the *Ranger*, who had driven a vehicle off its flight deck. By 0141, the lucky sailor was brought aboard the *Hamner* by Boatswain's Mate First Class Fred Simpson. Simpson was awarded the Navy and Marine Corps Medal for his part in this heroic rescue. The remainder of December was spent on Yankee Station with various carrier groups.

Departing the carrier group on January 2, 1968 to relieve a fleet ocean tug holding surveillance over a Russian trawler while the tug obtained replenishments at Da Nang, *Hamner* lost steering control from the bridge. Using after-steering, *Hamner* stayed on station until relieved the next day.

Badly in need of upkeep, *Hamner* returned to Subic Bay on January 4, 1968 for fifteen days maintenance. There she tied alongside the USS *Klondike* (AR-22) before returning to the Military Region I (MRI) Corps area for NGFS action. Arriving January 23 in the Corps area where some fifty thousand North Vietnamese troops had concentrated around the cities of Hue and Da Nang, *Hamner* relieved the USS *Chandler* (DD-717) of her duty station, then proceeded north to Da Nang and engaged in NGFS involving amphibious landings just below the DMZ, separating North from South Vietnam.

Between the twenty-sixth and thirty-first, *Hamner* was fifteen miles north of Chu Lai, engaged in NGFS with spotters reporting excellent target coverage against Viet Cong storage areas, bunkers, troop concentrations, and fortified artillery positions. During this period, *Hamner* was replenished at sea by the USS *Katmai* (AE-16), taking aboard over twenty-five hundred rounds. Each time while replenishing, she was relieved from the gunline by the cruiser USS *Newport News* (CA-148). On January 31, 1968, the North Vietnamese ignored the truce they had promised to uphold during the Lunar New Year (Tet) and took the war into the urban areas of South Vietnam, attacking major cities and US forces. The *Tet Offensive* had begun.

On February 1, 1968, having taken aboard some two thousand rounds from the USS *Mount Baker* (AE-4), *Hamner* returned to her NGFS assignment. On the second, she fired 913 rounds in support of 345 marines ashore taken under fire by enemy mortars, inflicting 141 casualties on the enemy. By day's end, mounts 51 and 52 gun barrels had blistered, and the destroyer had rendezvoused with the USS *Neches* (AO-47) for refueling. That same day, grateful spotters ashore sent *Hamner* a message that read, "Magnificent job, well done."

The third of February found *Hamner*, the USS *Richard S. Edwards* (DD-950), and the cruiser *Newport News* (CA-148) engaged in counter-battery. All ships returned enemy fire and silenced the shore's batteries. Some 536 rounds of ammunition were fired that day. Rendezvousing with the USS *Aludra* (AF-55) at 1800, *Hamner* replenished her grocery needs.

February 4 and 5 were spent on harassment and interdiction missions, firing at various targets with excellent coverage. A total of 705 rounds of ammunitions were fired during these two days.

On February 6, *Hamner* fired 382 rounds of ammunition at various targets, and by 1100, had left the northern MRI Corps area to proceed sixty miles south to the central MRI Corps area. Before leaving, marine spotters sent a message to the ship commending

Hamner for an outstanding job the past eleven days and for always being ready and on target.

Having replenished on the seventh of February (one thousand rounds taken aboard) from the USS *Fire Drake* (AE-14), *Hamner* fired one hundred sixty-five rounds of ammunition at Viet Cong positions around the city of Hue that day. And from February 8 to 11, she expended two thousand ninety rounds at enemy targets involving harassment and interdiction assignments. During this period, she was refueled by the USS *Tulagi* (AO-62) and the USS *Mattaponi* (AO-41), and replenished by the USS *Mount Katmai* (AE-16) and the USS *Vesuvius* (AE-15).

The morning of February 16, 1968 was a day for which the crew had long been waiting. On that morning, *Hamner* fired 321 rounds before departing the war zone. Her spotters reported excellent coverage. At 0630, the destroyer was relieved from NGFS at the DMZ and steamed for Subic Bay. She carried a very tired and weary crew.

Hamner had fired 7,298 rounds during the final twenty days of that period (January 21 through February 16) in the Tet Offensive, consistently earning the praise of spotters and of the naval command.

After returning to Subic Bay for three days of upkeep, *Hamner* departed for Australia on February 21. Nearing the equator, Neptune Rex and his gang boarded *Hamner*, demanding to know why there were "so many violations leading to captain's mast, excessive requests for liberty, and repeated bouts of seasickness" among the crew. Again, in accordance with tradition, a day was set aside when crossing the equator for shellbacks to initiate the slimy pollywogs into the ancient and sacred order of the deep. As a consequence, February 23, 1968 proved to be a trying day for some 248 pollywogs and a great day for the 30 shellbacks who carried out the tradition.

Skirting coral reefs, *Hamner* sailed into Darwin, Australia, for refueling and then steamed for the coal mining town of Wollongong (New South Whales, Australia) for a few days of well-earned rest and relaxation. After a very brief greeting by anti-war protesters, her crew went ashore from March 2 and 7 and thoroughly enjoyed five days of unmatched liberty.

Departing Australia on March 7 for the States, the destroyer stopped at Pago Pago, Tutuila Islands (American Samoa), and Pearl Harbor, Hawaii while en route to San Diego.

Throughout the cruise, when afforded the opportunity ashore, *Hamner*'s softball team, the Hawks, was the best in the fleet. Playing against the teams of the United States naval vessels, *Buck* (DD-761), *Klondike* (AD-22), *Orleck* (DD-886), *King* (DLG-10), *Passumpsic* (AO-107), *Mason* (DE-509), and even the coast guard cutter *Androscoggin* (WPG-68), the *Hamner* won eight out of twelve games.

Hamner arrived in San Diego on March 23, 1968. Leave and upkeep followed, and by April 23, *Hamner* once again commenced local operations involving ship duties and ASW schooling and assessment of her condition and readiness for combat. Throughout the month of July, she was tied alongside the USS *Dixie* (AD-14) for tender availability, and on August 1, proceeded to the San Francisco Naval Shipyard (Hunter's Point) for overhaul.

During presentations at the shipyard on October 11, *Hamner* was awarded the battle Efficiency E, Engineering E, Gunnery E, and the ASW A.

On December 3, 1968, *Hamner* steamed for her home port, San Diego, and at year-end, was tied alongside the tender USS *Piedmont* (AD-17).

Ammo Handling Frank "Moose" Magistro on left (dark hardhat)

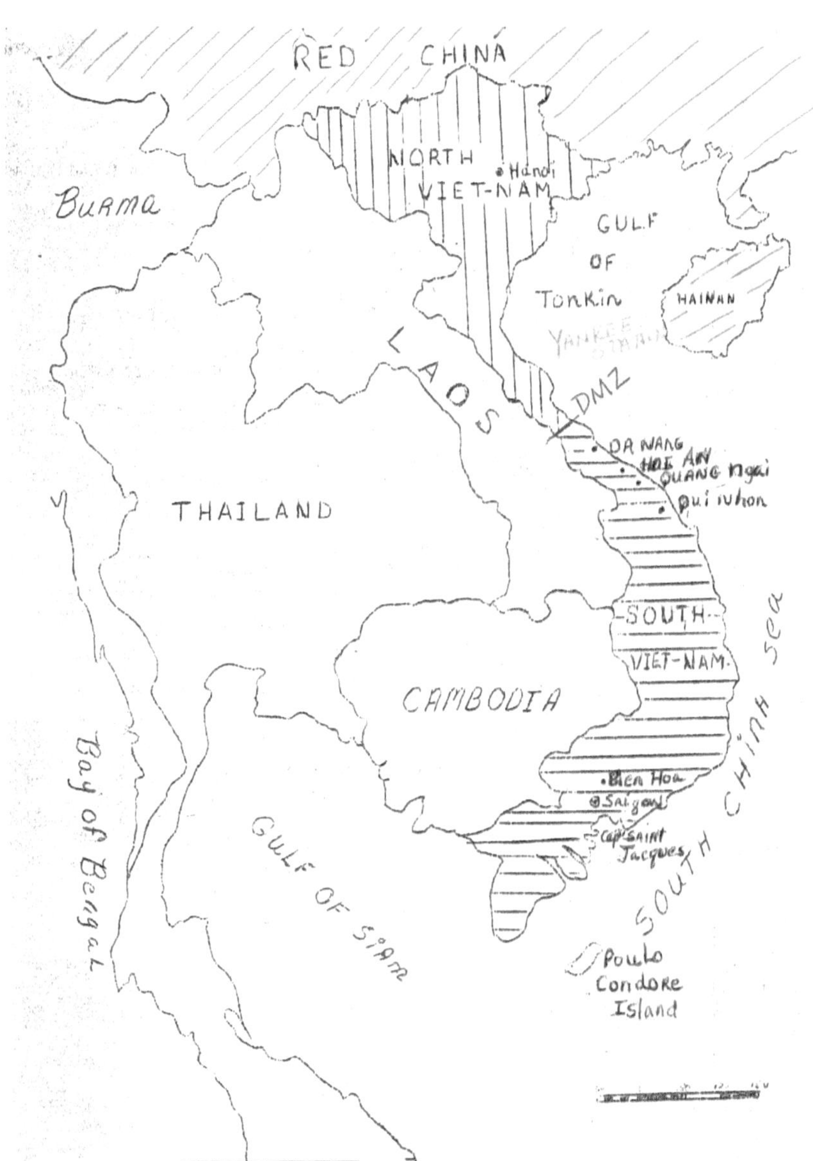

Copy of map from Hamner records

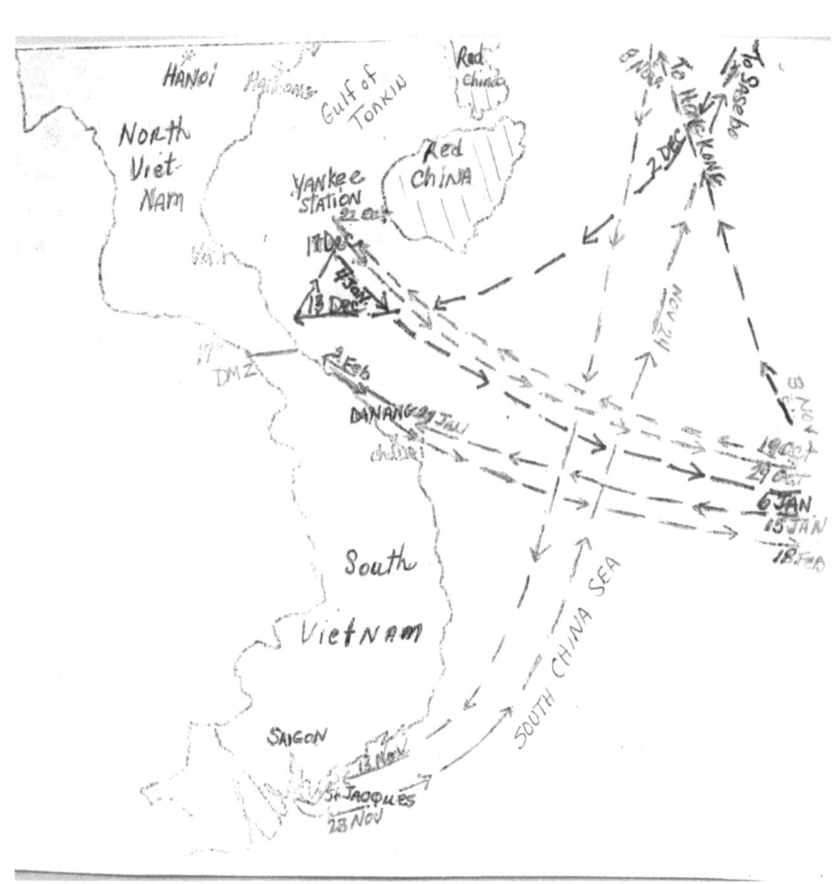

Hamner's cruise—October 1967 thru February 1968

Allen Geddes 1968

William Golder 1965-69

Ashley Gray 1967-69

Merrill Hathaway 1967-69

CHAPTER 10

General Quarters, 1969–1971

Having undergone yard repairs, training, and gunnery exercises throughout the better part of 1968 and well into 1969, *Hamner* was preparing for duty in the Far East. But before leaving San Diego in June 1969, a very significant addition was made to the *Hamner* because of the Navy's concern about the growing threat of surface missiles to destroyers, such as the Soviet Styx missile, which had been launched by Egyptian patrol boats to sink the *Eilat* in October 1967. A Ship Anti-Missile Integrated Defense (SAMID) ECM system was installed on the *Hamner*. SAMID used aluminum chaff-filled rockets as decoys to confuse a surface missile's radar guidance. The SAMID systems were gradually removed from the thirteen Gearing class destroyers on which they were installed, and this was after the January 1973 cease-fire in Vietnam.

Departing San Diego in June 1969, she headed westward for deployment in the South China Sea. Operating off South Vietnam, *Hamner* spent many hours in the Tonkin Gulf as a plane guard and watching for MiGs off Tiger Island. *Hamner* positioned herself just off the entrance of the Song-Ong-Doc River, and for four days, spent twenty-four hours around the clock in naval gunfire support (NGFS) of American Forces. From September 29 through October 1, 1969, *Hamner* and USS *John Craig* (DD-885) were involved in a SAR for a C-2A Greyhound (carrying as many as thirty-nine passengers in addition to its crew) which had crashed at sea on the way to the USS

Constellation (CV-64). Despite arriving on the scene shortly after the crash, the *Hamner* found almost no wreckage and no survivors. The crew was saddened when they found out a ship's steward, Viado, was lost in this accident.[10]

Hamner returned to the States in November 1969.

On September 8, 1970, after ten months of training exercises out of San Diego, and with an almost complete change over in officers and enlisted personnel, the destroyer was once again underway for the Far East. Steaming to the Hawaiian Islands where she took on fuel and stores, *Hamner* set course south by southwest and navigated her way toward the South Pacific.

Captain to navigator: "Plot a course to Auckland, New Zealand, and avoid the equator."

"Captain! Sir, that is not possible. Why do you want to avoid latitude zero-zero degree?"

"Because Neptunus Rex and his high tribunal are waiting there for pollywogs like me!"

Sailing at longitude 165-47W and latitude zero-zero degrees on 21 September 1970, sailors gathered on the helicopter flight deck as slimy pollywogs were tried, convicted, and punished for their impolite intrusion into the realm of Neptunus Rex. Once again, her crew became shellback-strong, captain and all.

Having crossed the equator, she sailed to Pago Pago for refueling. "Don't miss the Pago cable lift ride, and remember, the policemen wear kilts," crewmen were told as liberty was granted. Upon refueling (taking aboard 116,432 gallons of oil), along with the USS *Knox* (DE-1082), *Hamner* was once again on her way.

Continuing her southward journey, the crew trained in everything from damage control, to caring for vital machinery in the engineering spaces, including signaling and how to fix the shipboard Coke machine.

---

[10] Two *Hamner* crewmen actually lost their lives in 1969. In early 1969, with only a few days left to serve in the United States Navy, a crew member was killed when he was accidentally caught in the capstan during a mooring operation in San Diego.

On September 28, 1970, it was, "Hello, Auckland," as sailors watched miniskirts in the rain. The Occidental Pub and left-hand driving were something new for the crew to see! Before departing Auckland, *Hamner* participated for ten days in operation "LONGEX-70," a joint anti-submarine warfare and anti-aircraft gunnery operation involving naval ships of New Zealand, Australia, and Great Britain before steaming for the Philippines, stopping while en route at Manus Island (Admiralty Islands).

By late October, *Hamner* was back in Subic Bay preparing for her next assignment, and by November 17, the destroyer was en route to Kaohsiung, Taiwan, arriving on the twentieth. Sailors soon learned the port city of Kaohsiung rivaled that of Auckland for good times. The Tsoying Officers Club and the Sea Dragon were kept busy with the crew of *Hamner*, and the friendliness of the people and beautiful local scenery were well appreciated. Reluctantly, *Hamner* departed on the twenty-fifth for Yankee Station and flight operations with the USS *Hancock* (CVA-19) in the Tonkin Gulf before returning to Subic Bay on December 10.

On December 11, *Hamner* departed Subic Bay heading north for the US naval base at Yokosuka, Japan, where it docked at Pier 3. It was a great Christmas reunion as wives of *Hamner* crewmen were flown to Japan. The *Hamner* wives were part of a larger group that arrived via a special charter flight. At the time, under new policies naval operations provided charter transportation for wives to visit their husbands deployed at numerous overseas areas.

Leaving Yokosuka Harbor on December 29, 1970, *Hamner* steamed to Buckner Bay, Okinawa, where she refueled and headed for the Tonkin Gulf and duty on Yankee Station in support of American carriers whose aircraft were pounding North Vietnamese forces. By January 19, 1971, she was providing NGFS in the Military Region IX (MRIS) Corps area near Song Ba, South Vietnam. The short time on the gunline was well spent. *Hamner* fired a total of 256 rounds and received no counter-battery fire. Operating off South Vietnam, she didn't grab many headlines or suffer any casualties, but her crew spent many sleepless nights at General Quarters watching radar scopes, standing bridge watches, and experiencing the multitude of sensations halfway around the world that earlier crews had experienced. Whether on patrol or involved in NGFS of American forces who were hammering away at communist positions, they took care of their weaponry and did their job consistently, one day at a time, in the Tonkin Gulf. Having concluded her gunline duties, *Hamner* returned to Subic Bay on the sixteenth where she moored at Rivera Pier Berth 14/15.

On January 22, 1971, *Hamner* was underway with the USS *Chicago* (CLG-11) for duties in the positive identification radar advisory zone (PIRAZ) in the Tonkin Gulf. While on station and making a replenishment, she approached the USS *Camden* (AOE-2), and the two ships had a minor collision with each other. The results were two minor punctures of the bow well above the waterline, anchor damage to one anchor.

By early February, *Hamner* was back in Subic Bay. While in port, fourth-grade students from Subic's Binictican elementary school had their look at a real fighting ship when they toured *Hamner*, and later invited numerous *Hamner* crewmen to a Valentine's Day party at their school.

Departing Subic Bay on February 13, 1971, *Hamner* steamed for Hong Kong, where on the fifteenth, she moored at buoy 3. A typical day of liberty in Hong Kong for her crew included a tram ride to Victoria Peak, a visit to Tiger Balm Gardens, a Star Ferry ride across the Harbor to Kowloon, which was just a whisper away from Communist China. Mary Soo's hull painting of *Hamner* was the crowning point of the visit as *Hamner* departed the city on February 22.

Entering Subic Bay on February 23, *Hamner* moored at the NAVMAG to off-load ammunition. A total of 302 projectiles and 744 powder cartridges were off-loaded. After off load, *Hamner* moored to Alava Piers 7 and 8, and evening liberty was granted.

The next morning, *Hamner* was underway for San Diego via Guam, Midway Island, and Pearl Harbor with the destroyer USS *Rowan* (DD-782). That afternoon, two stowaways were discovered. Both were shore based in Subic and were on a restricted status there. On arrival at Guam, *Hamner* moored and commenced refueling.

Both stowaways were removed by guard at Guam. Afterward, the crew was granted three hours of liberty to enjoy the island. Most of the crew congregated at the mobile canteen, which was offering its service at pier side.

By early March, having refueled, *Hamner* departed Guam, setting a northeast course for Midway Island where she again refueled (four hours of liberty were granted) before departing for Pearl Harbor. On liberty in Honolulu, her crew attended hula dance parties, ate McDonald's burgers, and watched "hippie girls of the times" singing "Lovely Hula Hands."

Hamner returned to the US naval station, San Diego, on March 12, 1971, docking at Pier 3, and commenced a thirty-day personnel stand-down (50 percent of the crew were permitted leave). A happy day for her crew.

Robert Frey 1969-71

James Hall 1969-71

USS Biddle (DLG-34)

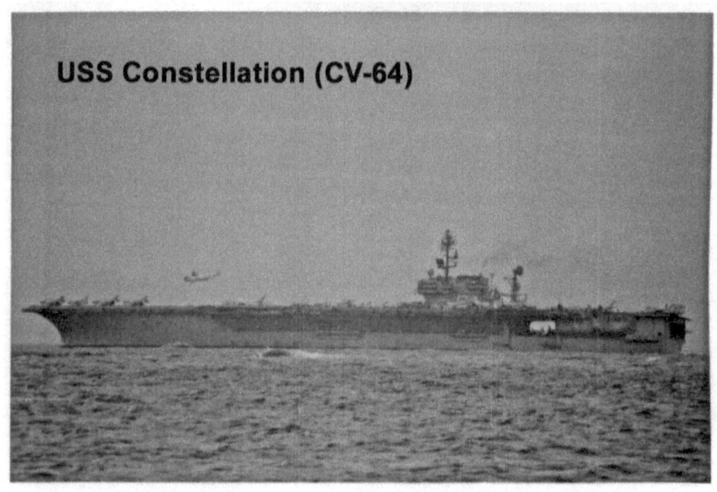

USS Constellation (CV-64)

This is NOT a drill 1969

Lower the Whaleboat...

We are heading to Kaohsiung!

Refueling at sea

CHAPTER 11

"Dragon Wagon" Guns
A-blazin', 1972

"Sailor! What is the state of the sea?"

"Sir, the state of the sea is when you have liberty and no boats, or boats and no liberty."

"What is the current state?"

"Liberty and no money, sir."

Stateside liberty was nearing an end for the next eight months as *Hamner*'s crew prepared for her next WestPac cruise.

February 8, 1972 was a characteristic San Diego day. The sky was clear and warm with an affable sun shining down. At the US Naval Station, Pier 1, it was also a typical morning. Another destroyer was on her way to WestPac. Underway at around 1000, the USS *Hamner* slid quietly beneath the Coronado Bay Bridge and past Ballast Point as she headed for Pearl Harbor and points west. The sleek, grey hull was winding her way toward the Orient, carrying proud tradition, encompassing nineteen consecutive WestPac cruises. Passing buoy 1-SD, there was not a crewman aboard who could begin to foresee the outcome of a most rigorous and exciting deployment. As *Hamner* steamed westward, and the sun's reflection dimmed on Point Loma, many of her young crewmen felt the thrill of the unknown.

As previous crew had experienced, *Hamner* passed through the San Bernardino Strait and found it infested with the hazards of numerous small craft and dangerous shoal waters. Entering Subic Bay on March 1, 1972, *Hamner* moored at the ammunition and fuel piers to fill her magazines and top off her fuel tanks. Before the remote daydreams of liberty could be translated into reality, *Hamner* was underway to participate in special operations the following morning, heading toward Mindanao as backup for the Philippine government's insurgency operation in the southern islands, then returning on the fifth.

On March 6–11, *Hamner* moored in Subic Bay. As previous crews had experienced, Subic Bay seemed to be a South Pacific paradise with palm trees, coconuts, sandy beaches, blue ocean, a cool native breeze, and the city of Olongapo.

Departing Subic Bay in a glistening wake on March 12, she sped toward her initial gunline assignment in Vietnam's Four Corps Military Region areas. Arriving on the fourteenth at the Military Region IV (MRIV) Corps area, *Hamner* immediately engaged in twenty-four-hour naval gunfire bombardment against enemy position ashore. Completing her naval gunfire support (NGFS) assignment, she sped on to relieve the destroyer escort USS *Sample* (DE-1048). *Hamner* was greeted by a fiery tropical sun baking the south western coast of Vietnam. Leaving the gulf of Siam two weeks later on the twenty-seventh, *Hamner* made preparations for her next assignment in the Military Region I (MRI) Corps area.

Even off the coast of Vietnam as her bow methodically slashed through the sea, the sound of old paint being chipped away was never-ending, for the *Hamner's* hardworking crew always tried to keep her spick-and-span.

Operating off the windswept strand near the city of Quảng Trị, from April 1 to 4 1972, NGFS of the MRI Corps area was quite a different experience from that of MRIV Corps. Depending heavily upon the growing naval armada and its NGFS to blast enemy positions, the embattled defenders of Quảng Trị, surrounded by North Vietnamese, held their ground. Keeping her guns firing and dodging concentrated enemy fire during this period, *Hamner* came to the rescue of downed pilot First Lt. Richard Abbott, USAF. *Hamner's* baptism of fire prepared her well for the next upcoming assignment.

From April 5 to 23, *Hamner* was a charter member of Operation Freedom Train, whose mission was to strike surface-to-air-missile (SAM) sites along the North Vietnamese coastline with naval gunfire bombardments. April 16 typified the tempo of operations and skill with which her crew operated. In a coordinated surface air strike mission, naval forces struck a daring blow on Haiphong Harbor. On April 16, 1972, *Hamner*, under withering hostile fire, steamed into the heavily fortified harbor with all guns a blazing to rescue CDR. D. L. Moss, commanding officer of carrier attack squadron VA-94, USS *Coral Sea* (CVA-43). The commander's crusader aircraft had been heavily damaged by ground fire, requiring him to eject over the harbor. He was successfully returned to the *Coral Sea* later that day. In the midst of these grueling conditions, *Hamner*, known to the US fleet as the Dragon Wagon, continued the legacy of proudly projecting American naval power across the Pacific Ocean.

One early April morning, while steaming toward an assigned mission, she encountered two contacts tentatively identified by radar as North Vietnamese PT boats. After the *Hamner* fired a few salvos, the targets rapidly disappeared. Later evaluation indicated the targets most likely were only ghost images that frequent radar in the tropical interface. By mid-month, *Hamner* joined up with task force 77.1 comprised of USS *Buchanan* (DDG-14), USS *Oklahoma City* (CCG-5), and herself. Their task was to bombard "lighters" loaded with war materials taken aboard from freighters (presumably Communist Chinese) southwest of Hon La Island (thirty miles northwest of the port city of Dong Hoi). On April 24, *Hamner* became part of Operation North Star whose mission was sea-air rescue. Finishing April with a 100 percent operating tempo and firing over five thousand rounds, *Hamner* sped for a well-deserved respite to Subic Bay on May 3, 1972.

Departing Subic Bay on May 16 for special operations, the crew prepared themselves for the extra strain and stress they knew their new assignment would demand. By May 18, *Hamner* was off the Vietnamese coast hammering away day and night at enemy targets as part of operation Linebacker. Leaving the operation on May 29, 1972, *Hamner* became part of Operation North Star and remained on this assignment until June 10, when she returned to the MRI

Corps area and participated in NGFS until departing for Subic Bay on June 15.

Leaving Subic Bay on June 25, *Hamner* proceeded back to the MRI Corps gunline, engaging in NGFS until July 5. On July 6, she became part of the NGFS involving Operation Linebacker until the fifteenth. Thereafter, *Hamner* found herself re-gunning (after firing over ten thousand rounds) with new five-inch barrels in Da Nang, Vietnam, before returning to Subic Bay on the eighteenth.

Departing Subic Bay on July 19 for Hong Kong, *Hamner* navigated the circuitous channel into bejeweled Hong Kong Harbor on the twentieth. The panoply of East and West struck the haggard crewmen with awe as their eyes glistened with excitement and adventure.

Departing Hong Kong on July 27, *Hamner* was assigned plane guard duty with the USS *Saratoga* (CVA-60) until August 16, before returning overnight to Subic Bay on the nineteenth. Departing Subic Bay on August 20, *Hamner* proceeded to Yankee Station and plane guard duty with the USS *Oriskany* (CVA-34) until August 31 before returning to Subic Bay for the tortuous waiting for *out-chop* to begin.

On September 7, 1972, the dreams of *Hamner's* crew materialized with the final *out-chop* from Subic Bay and the setting of a course for the States, with refueling stops at Midway Island and Pearl Harbor, Hawaii.

As *Hamner's* deployment drew to a tortuously slow conclusion in September, her salty crewmen would never forget the nostalgia that made life bearable for them. There was not one crewman aboard who would ever forget what *Hamner* and her shipmates had done, and what *Hamner* and these shipmates meant to her during the deployment. Unlike WestPac cruises of the past, she was on the gunline most of the time, never making ports of call to Japan, Australia, or Taiwan. Throughout the cruise, *Hamner* expended 12,130 rounds of ammunition and received over 500 rounds of hostile fire. *Hamner* replenished at sea (fuel, ammunition, and stores) ninety times and cruised 57,147 miles, burning 3,766,530 gallons of fuel. September 27, 1972 was a happy day in San Diego when the boatswains mate called out, "Moored, Shift Colors!"

The word was passed, the sailors were home at last!

The "Dragon Wagon" in Action 1972

Hong Kong Harbor 1972

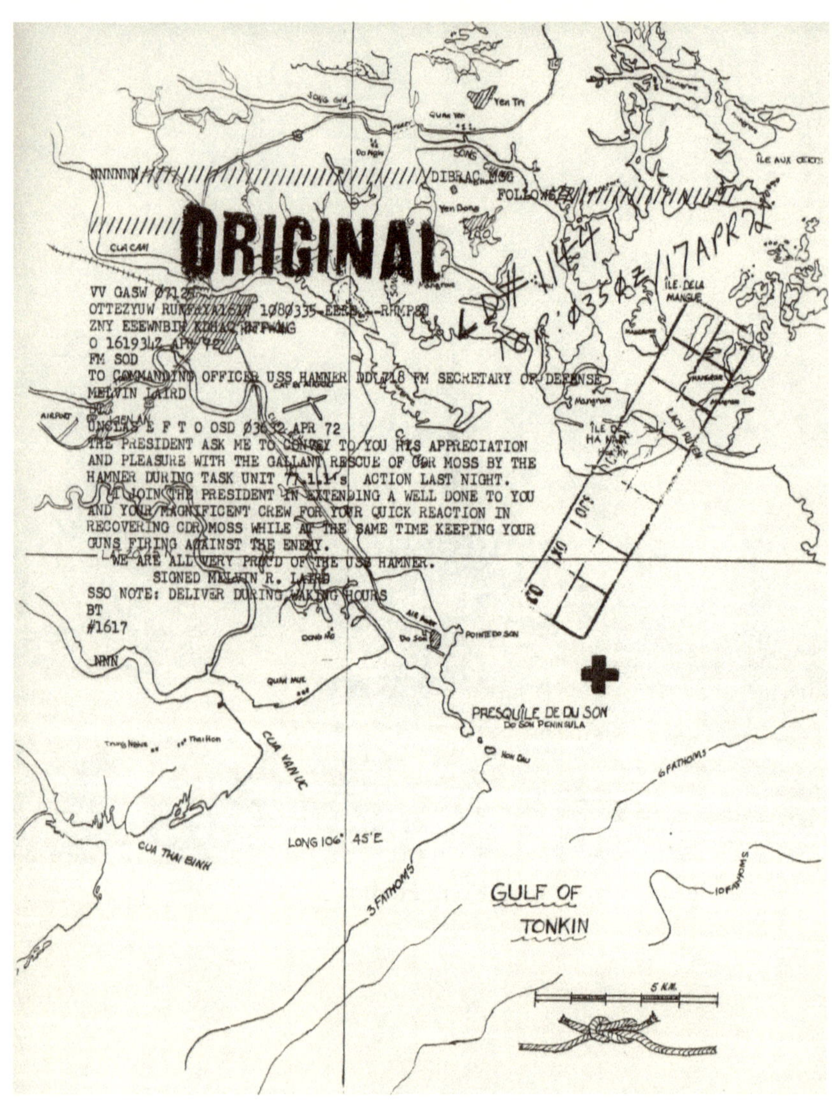

Communication from the President on 1972 Rescue

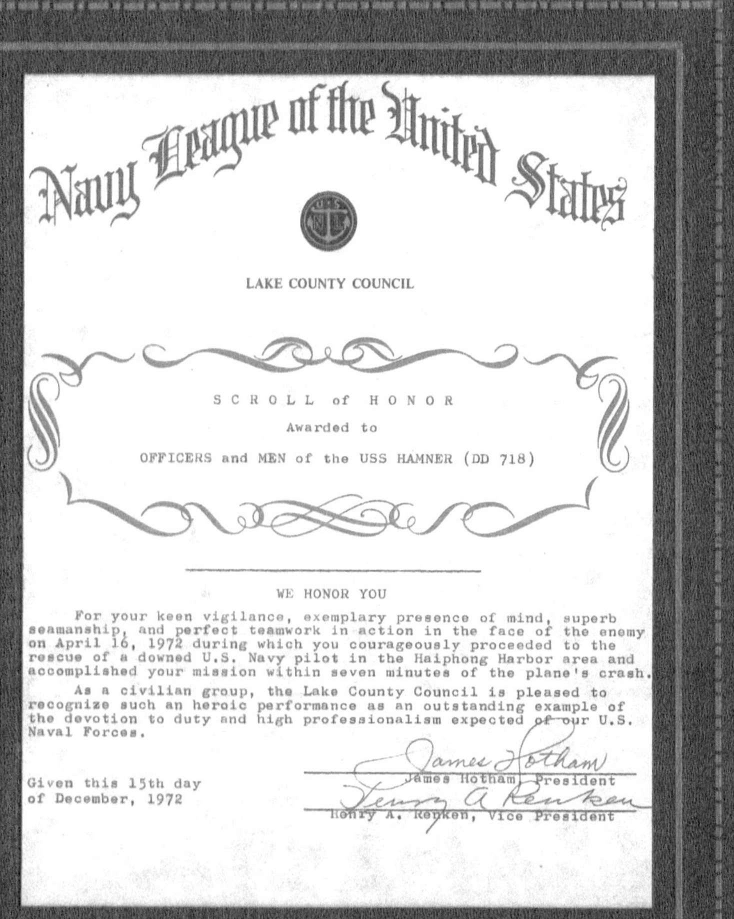

Navy League of the United States

LAKE COUNTY COUNCIL

SCROLL of HONOR
Awarded to
OFFICERS and MEN of the USS HAMNER (DD 718)

WE HONOR YOU

For your keen vigilance, exemplary presence of mind, superb seamanship, and perfect teamwork in action in the face of the enemy on April 16, 1972 during which you courageously proceeded to the rescue of a downed U.S. Navy pilot in the Haiphong Harbor area and accomplished your mission within seven minutes of the plane's crash.

As a civilian group, the Lake County Council is pleased to recognize such an heroic performance as an outstanding example of the devotion to duty and high professionalism expected of our U.S. Naval Forces.

Given this 15th day
of December, 1972

James Hotham, President
Henry A. Renken, Vice President

Ship Saves Downed Pilot   Chicago Today – Wednesday, April 19, 1972

Daring Haiphong Rescue

WASHINGTON (AP)– A United States destroyer, its guns blazing, sailed into the mouth of Haiphong harbor on April 16 to rescue a downed Navy pilot, it has been disclosed here, and President Nixon has congratulated the Ships Crew.

The rescue was made during the heaviest raids on North Viet Nam.

Testifying before the Senate Foreign Relations Committee yesterday, Secretary of Defense Melvin R. Laird, a World War II destroyer man himself, praised the exploit of the destroyer Hamner in picking up the pilot of an A7 attack plane only seven minutes after it was downed, one of two U.S. planes lost in the raids. The pilot was identified as Comdr. David Lee. Moss a squadron leader from San Francisco.

Message to: Crew U.S.S. Hamner DD-718
(The John Wayne of the Pacific)
From: President Richard M. Nixon

Well done to a magnificent crew for your quick reaction in recovering Comdr. David Moss while at the same time keeping your guns firing against the enemy.

From Ship's Log

9570 Wilshire Blvd, Suite 408
Beverly Hills, California 90212
August 13, 1976

Men of the U.S.S. Hamner D.D. 718
C/O Commander Robert W. Brune
FPO San Francisco, California 96601

Dear Men of the U.S.S. Hamner:

A cousin of the young Annapolis graduate of World War II in whose memory your ship was named told me of a privileged visit that he had aboard your ship by a Navy invitation extended as a courtesy to the family. I was told that because of her actions off Indo – China during the Viet Nam affair that she was unofficially dubbed " The John Wayne." I want you to know that I am complimented even though it was said in humor.

Your Log shows that you had a heroic Command of Officers and Men during the war years and I am sure a fine peace time morale, though I presume your duties seem less dramatic; and like some of the other branches of our Armed Forces, not fully understood.

May I as one of many millions of Americans offer our Armed Forces a hearty salute. My compliments and congratulations.

Sincerely

John Wayne

JW/os

From Ship's records

CHAPTER 12

Running the Columbia River, 1972–1975

Returning to San Diego from WestPac in September 1972, the USS *Hamner*, after several months of stand-down while her crew took leave, sailed at year-end to Willamette Shipyards (Richmond, California) for a complete overhaul. Here, *Hamner* was converted from burning black oil (Navy special fuel oil) to naval distillate (diesel oil). Having completed the overhaul, she was assigned to the Naval Reserve Force-Pacific (NRF-P) on July 1, 1973, whereupon *Hamner* was transferred from her home port of San Diego (after twenty-seven years) to Treasure Island Naval Station, San Francisco, California, becoming part of Destroyer Squadron 31. Her days as a combatant destroyer serving with the fleet in the line of fire were over. She now served as a training platform for naval reservists. By summer's end in 1973, *Hamner* made her first cruise with reservists to Hawaii, and in June 1974, she again sailed to the islands with reservists for two months training before returning to Todd Shipyards, Alameda, California.

In early 1975, *Hamner's* operating port was shifted from Treasure Island to nearby Alameda Naval Station, California. On the day the Vietnamese War came to an end, April 30, 1975, *Hamner* and her crew were busy preparing to enter dry dock in the month of June at the naval station. Coming out of dry dock, orders were received from the Department of the Navy reassigning her to DesRon-37 located at the Navy and Marine Corps Reserve Center (Swan Island), Portland, Oregon. There, *Hamner's* primary task was to train naval reservists in standard shipboard operations.

Departing Alameda by the end of August 1975, *Hamner* got underway, steaming for deep waters of the Pacific Ocean. Passing beneath the Golden Gate Bridge and setting a northerly course with a standard operating speed of twelve knots, *Hamner* steamed to her new duty station. How little did her crew realize that reaching Portland from the ocean was a treacherous piloting task (particularly in winter months) for any ship, since some 120 miles of the Columbia River had to be navigated to reach the city, not to mention Swan Island.

Holding steerageway in the vicinity of the "CR" buoy some two miles off the Columbia River bar (where the mouth of the river meets the ocean), a civilian bar pilot licensed by the United States Coast Guard (USCG) boarded from an oceangoing tug. The pilot then assisted in navigating the vessel past the shifting sand bar to the city of Astoria, Oregon, some seventeen miles upstream. There the first pilot disembarked and was replaced by another river pilot who guided the destroyer the remaining distance. The pilots, assigned by federal law to guide ships up and down the river, were specially trained in awareness of hazards, including all ongoing river dredging operations, and were experts on river navigation.

Steaming up the Columbia River (early in September 1975) for the first time was a new experience for the crew. Boats followed with signs welcoming the destroyer to the northwest, and there were people on the docks of the towns along the river, with huge banners, waving. The welcome was so great that by the time *Hamner* arrived at the beautiful city of Portland, situated at the at the confluence of the Willamette and Columbia Rivers, including the majestic volcanic mountains (Mount Saint Helens and Mount Hood), the crew all thought they "had died and gone to hog heaven!"

As a port city, Portland offered a haven for the reservist crew who would be trained while aboard. City lights twinkled with night life, and the reservists could always find a warm place out of the rain to eat along the riverfront before returning to duty. At the time, *Hamner* had a crew of some 60 percent regular and 40 percent reservists. Rents were low for regular crewmen as the University of Portland was less than two miles away with many apartments available. As for the reservists, many lived in the Portland area and commuted to the destroyer for weekend duty.

With her mooring lines taken in by 0600 on the morning of October 10, 1975, *Hamner* was underway, destined for gunnery training exercises off San Clemente Island, California, accompanied by a USCG licensed river pilot. At the time, how little did the crew know the perilous time they were about to experience. Steaming down the Willamette to the Columbia River started uneventful. Lookouts were posted to keep a keen eye open for drifting logs which were deadly as any live torpedo, and to watch for commercial fishing boats including recreational boats.

As *Hamner* continued her downriver voyage, fog began to set in.

"Captain," the quartermaster said.

"Yes, quartermaster?"

"I recommend we slow to five knots. It is becoming difficult to navigate with the fog as it is."

"Very well."

"Officer of the deck, reduce speed to five knots."

"Aye, aye, Captain," the OOD replied before giving the command, "Slow to five knots."

"Pilot, have we reached the confluence of the Willamette and Columbia?"

"Captain, we should be coming on CG buoy 47 at the confluence any time. Also, Kelly Point should be in sight. I recommend you maintain the present heading and speed."

"Officer of the Deck, commence sounding the fog signal at regular intervals."

"Aye, aye, Captain."

"Bridge, CIC here, we have radar contact of a possible small craft off the starboard beam, one thousand yards, bearing 0270 degrees."

"Very well."

Continuing her long voyage toward the Pacific, *Hamner* navigated the precarious river waters, avoiding commercial freighters and ferry boats, as the pilot made recommendations to the skipper involving the best course and deep-water channels to follow. Some six hours after getting underway, the fog had lifted, and she was now nearing the Pacific coast. Incoming coast guard weather reports indicated gale force winds (thirty to forty knots) were in effect along the Oregon coast. Arriving at the last port town along the river (Astoria, Oregon), the river pilot disembarked at CG buoy 17 as the sand bar pilot boarded to assist in guiding *Hamner* the remaining seventeen miles through the upper and lower Desdemona shoal to the Pacific Ocean.

"Captain. The Columbia river bar is one of the most treacherous stretches of water in the world. We are not going to attempt to navigate through the bar during slack water," began the sand bar pilot. "Because we are running late out of Portland, we will enter the bar with a strong ebb current augmented by river runoff which is an extremely dangerous time to be caught on the bar. Worse still, the bar has its own mind, and tidal currents may gain tremendous velocity due to the river runoff. You can expect steep waves fifteen to twenty feet at one- to two-minute intervals."

"Understood, pilot."

As *Hamner* continued her northerly transit through the bar while being battered by giant swells, her crew could see hulls of capsized ships that didn't make it, buried in the sand, reminding them of the strength of the bar.

"Captain, the rudder is not responding because we are tossing and turning. Sir, the currents are pushing us broadside toward the bar, and we are broaching and pitching enough that our propellers are in the air. We are losing steerageway."

"Officer of the deck, flank speed."

"Aye, aye, flank speed."

"Captain, the rudder is slowly responding."

"Good, hold that helm steadfast at all costs, helmsman, don't lose it. We must transit this leg of the Desdemona Shoal before reaching the final 225-degree leg across the bar."

"Aye, aye, Captain."

"Lieutenant, this is my first river cruise. How often does this destroyer ply the river?"

"Sailor, twice a month rain, shine, or snow!"

"Oh, Mamma mia, Lieutenant. This river is ranked as one of the roughest in the world and is called the Graveyard of the Pacific. If it doesn't swallow us alive, once I get back ashore on liberty, I'm going to buy myself the largest mug of beer I can find and drink this river away."

"Sailor, I hear you."

As *Hamner* worked her way through the last perilous stretch, breaking free to sail the deep ocean waters she knew so well, a CG tug came alongside and picked up the pilot, returning him to a large tanker heavily anchored one mile offshore where USCG licensed pilots come and go to work each day.

Having reached the gunnery exercise range off San Clemente Island, the gunnery officer ordered, "Commence firing the fore and aft mounts." As previous crew experienced, there was short pensive silence and then *Hamner*'s four five-inch guns roared simultaneously. The vessel would shudder, and the men in the mounts would see the guns blur as the recoil and spent casings were ejected.

From a target distance of four miles, *Hamner*'s projectiles reached their targets in fifteen seconds. Crewmen on the bridge peering through binoculars would feel heat on their faces from flames spewed by the gun nearest them, and the pungent smell of burnt gunpowder was always heavy in the air throughout the ship.

"Lieutenant, why is a ship referred to as 'she'?

"Sailor, a ship is always referred to as a 'she' because it costs so much to keep one in paint and powder."

There was always time for fun aboard the destroyer, even among the officers. Winning a Snickers candy bar was a great reward among them involving seamanship. If docking the destroyer could be accomplished without assistance of a tug, the OOD would be rewarded a Snickers bar. Should he require assistance, then his peers would snicker at him.

As an NRF-P training vessel, duty for many regulars was somewhat monotonous at times. *Hamner* would occasionally sail to ports such as Seattle, San Francisco, or San Diego where weekend reservists would board, and the regulars would assign them training tasks. When home ported, *Hamner* would go down the river on weekends for reservist training, steaming out on Saturday and returning Sunday. Not a fun trip for those who had sea or anchor details, as it took an average of seven hours to run the river one way. Her hardworking crew always looked forward to returning to Portland where they anxiously would await liberty call.

"Barmaid, I'll have the largest mug of beer you can serve."

"Sailor, this mug is on the house. THANK YOU FOR SERVING OUR COUNTRY."

Hamner 1973

Lawrence Beamer
1972-75

Charlie Robinson 1971-73

Lee Smoot 1975-77

CHAPTER 13

Boatswain Mate—Set the Deck Watch, 1976

The USS *Hamner* (DD-718) by 1976 was becoming a veteran at sailing the Columbia River with reservists aboard.[11]

As usual, the tight waters of the Desdemona Shoal at the mouth of the Columbia River were always difficult to navigate even with an experienced bar pilot aboard. Here at the mouth of the mightiest river flowing into the Pacific Ocean from the American continents, the Columbian ends its journey, and the Graveyard of the Pacific begins. Ships were strictly prohibited to navigate the river at night by USCG regulations. Given hours of steaming the river were always posted.

"Radio room. This is the captain. The seas are moderately heavy today and a coast guard cutter is coming alongside and will attempt to transfer a bar pilot aboard. Commence playing over the ships sound speakers the US Coast Guard hymn "Semper Paratus," and continue playing the hymn until the cutter departs."

---

[11] Euro-American exploration of the river began in 1775, when the Spanish explorer Bruno de Hecela sailed within sight of its mouth. Treacherous waves breaking over the river bar prevented him from entering. Nevertheless, he placed the river mouth on Spanish charts.

"Aye, aye, Captain." With the pilot leaping aboard and the hymn playing, each side saluted the other in a gesture of respect before the cutter pulled away.

Oh, Mamma mia, Lieutenant, sir, we just took a forty-three-degree roll and we are only at red buoy 22. What would happen if we keeled over?"

"Sailor, the US navy taught you how to swim, didn't they?"

Since there was no gunnery range off the Northwest coast, *Hamner* would often steam from Portland, to the Alameda Naval Station (near San Francisco) where liberty would be granted, and usually a few reservists from the area would come aboard, then she would continue on to San Clemente Island, some seventy nautical miles off San Diego, to conduct gunnery training exercises. At night, with *Hamner* bow slashing through the sea and her crew at General Quarters stations, night firing of the fore and aft twin five-inch guns' mounts would light up the skies and shake the destroyer from bow to stern as crew members watched in awe. As each gunnery exercise came to a close, the crew would go about retrieving all spent shell casings spewed about the deck and make ready for the next exercise. Upon completion of these exercises, *Hamner* usually sailed to San Diego where liberty would be granted before returning to Portland.

By mid-1976, the sleek naval greyhound, now well-seasoned at plying the river's treacherous currents, bridges, pilings, ferry boats, and sand bars, set sail from Swan Island. Passing Cape Disappointment to her starboard, *Hamner* started a cruise northward for Nanaimo, Canada, via Juan de Fuca Strait. Arriving at Nanaimo, located in Departure Bay, Vancouver Island, *Hamner's* crew made ready the gangplank to go ashore, when they realized the plank would not reach the pier landing. Experiencing a twenty-foot low tide, the crew rigged a wooden plank (that each sailor carefully walked) from the 01 deck (helo deck) to the landing, a tidal experience not to be forgotten by any of her crew.

With her new status as a Naval Force-Pacific training vessel, *Hamner* gave Neptunus Rex (and his rowdy gang) a break. The crew could now snooze at sea knowing she would never again attempt to cross the equator with slimy pollywogs.

"Lieutenant, sir. The west coast of Oregon is a wonderful place. It hails, it snows, and the spray freezes on your face. Any chance mess could send a hot cup of coffee to my bridge lookout station, sir?"

When docked, twenty-four-hour watches would be maintained on the quarterdeck and ongoing activities on or about the ship were monitored on the quarter deck. It was here that the yeoman's liberty cards could be obtained. Quarterdeck watches were manned by an officer and a petty officer, and during the day, a messenger was included. The quarterdeck provided shelter for those on watch from Oregon's, wind, snow, and rain. Occasionally (for training purposes), a pier sentry would be posted.

"Lieutenant, sir. Why do I have to salute the quarterdeck officers when boarding? I do salute the national ensign, but why do I have to salute you if you have watch on the quarterdeck? I don't salute you any other time on board."

"Sailor, the quarterdeck has been a "sacred" area from the earliest days of naval history. Saluting is an old and impressive custom of respect and obedience in recognition of the seat of authority within the ship held by the officer of the deck when boarding or leaving."

Knowing the mouth of the Columbia River was the "Graveyard of the Pacific" where almost two thousand vessels of all types and about seven hundred lives (including bar pilots) have been claimed by the treacherous waters of the Peninsula (Desdemona shoal) over the past three hundred years, *Hamner* relied on the bar pilot's knowledge and experience whether to cross the bar or not, since the bar can be as calm as a teacup at times. Then the tide changes. Millions of gallons of river water trying to get out suddenly meet millions of gallons of ocean trying to get in over a shallow bar. A wind comes up from the west or southwest, and the teacup becomes a wind-whipped, swirling white maelstrom in a matter of minutes. Suddenly, it's one of the most dangerous places on the ocean.

"Sailor, tell me what the scuttlebutt is."

"Sir, the scuttlebutt is a sailor's source of fresh drinking water. Also, a place to exchange rumors, sir."

"Sailor, what is the latest scuttlebutt?"

"We sail for British Columbia, Canada, at the break of day."

CHAPTER 14

Captain, Sir, Bar Pilot Boarding, 1977–1979

Stationed at the Navy and Marine Corps Reserve Center, Portland, Oregon, in 1977, and assigned to DesRon-37 (Navy Reserve Force) were the USS *Hamner* (DD-718), USS *Epperson* (DD-719), USS *Carpenter* (DD-825), USS *Theodore E. Chandler* (DD-717), USS *Ozbourn* (DD-846), USS *Rogers* (DD-876), USS *Wiltsie* (DD-716), USS *McKean* (DD-784), USS *Higbee* (DD-806), USS *Orleck* (DD-886), USS *Hollister* (DD-788), and the USS *Owen* (DD-827). These sleek naval greyhounds of the past were fast aging. Departing the Reserve Center would get underway with weekend reservists, navigating the Columbia River. Arriving at CG buoy 17 with Astoria, Oregon, to *Hamner*'s port, the river pilot disembarked, and the bar pilot boarded. Continuing her journey downriver toward the upper Desdemona Shoal, *Hamner* began experiencing fast-moving tidal currents and rough waves, creating problems.

"Bridge, damage control here. Inform the captain we are springing leaks fore and aft and are working at plugging them as best we can."

"Aye."

"Officer of the deck, bring her about. I am returning to the protective waters of Astoria where we will tie up overnight before returning to Portland."

"Aye, aye, Captain."

By midafternoon, *Hamner* had steamed easterly upriver approximately 110 miles, where she left the Columbia at the confluence of the Willamette River, then steamed another ten miles to the Reserve Center located a few miles northwest of Portland in a slough at Swan Island. Here she tied up at a pier that extended from the reserve center parking lot where other destroyers were berthed.

Navigating the river was a difficult task. Steaming downstream, *Hamner* had to make a speed greater than the river flow in order to maintain steerage. Spring runoffs swelled the river and increased its flow rate, causing more problems. Steaming upriver was much easier since *Hamner* could transit at a much slower speed and easily maintain steerage.

Underway for sea operations in 1977, some of her crew got the brilliant idea to see if they could make a kite that would be able to take the force of wind while underway. Finding some canvas, old welding sticks, and rope used in making lifeline netting, they made the kite and decided it would be fun to fly it from the fantail. It wasn't long before the captain, standing on a bridge wing spotted the kite and proceeded to chew out the sailors for not manning their gun mount 52 station during a reserve fleet training exercise. No one was written up, but the captain was not happy.

When at sea, off-duty hours for the crew had not changed much from those experienced by previous crew members in earlier years. The former (OH-1) Drone Anti-Submarine Helicopter hangar was used as the crew lounge, having several soda machines, a TV, and lounge chairs. The crew used its flight deck for morning muster, an inside hangout at sea, and to smoke if the seas were too rough for smoking on the fantail. In port, it became the sundeck for those who were assigned weekend duty aboard.

With orders to participate in torpedo target testing, *Hamner* by mid-1977, with pilot aboard departed Portland. Steaming past the lower Desdemona Shoal bar into the Pacific, she encountered giant ocean swells as a coast guard tug came alongside, attempting to pick up the pilot. Pulling alongside in heavy seas, the tug time after time slammed into the *Hamner* in attempting to transfer the pilot. After numerous attempts were made, it was decided to ask for a coast guard helicopter transfer of the pilot. At the last minute, the pilot, wearing a life jacket, unexpectedly made a dangerous but successful ten-foot leap from *Hamner*'s deck out over open water onto the tug. Having rounded Cape Disappointment to her starboard side, *Hamner* set a course for Seattle where she was to be used as a target for torpedo testing. As her crew watched with excitement and caution, the first torpedo zipped beneath her bow as planned.

"Oh, Mamma mia. Lieutenant, sir, what would happen if those torpedoes got mixed up and a live one came at us?'

"Sailor, you are wearing your life jacket, aren't you?"

With the anchor detail and deck watch set (section one), *Hamner*, by early autumn 1977, was underway from Portland, navigating the river for the Pacific Ocean. Informed by the USCG that the river sand bar (Desdemona Shoal) was closed to all ship traffic because of heavy seas, *Hamner* decided to go into Astoria, Oregon, and tie up at the Thunderbird Motel pier. Once there, her plans were to continue crew training exercises at dockside as it waited word that the sand bar was open to traffic. As *Hamner* was maneuvering into port, *BOOM*!

"Officer of the deck, what was that?"

"Captain, sir. I believe we hit a submerged log."

"Bridge, engine room here. Our port propeller appears to be vibrating. We have vibration involving its shaft."

"Officer of the deck, have the engine room throttle the port engine to stop."

"Aye, aye, Captain."

"Captain, sir, we have throttled the port engine back. Vibration has stopped."

"Very well, maintain the starboard engine at ahead slow. We will dock and in the morning return to Swan Island."

Departing early the next morning, *Hamner* returned to the reserve center at Swan Island where arrangements were made to send her to Northwest Marine Ironworks at Portland for inspection. Once in dry dock, her port propeller was found to be bent and had to be replaced.

Underway at the break of dawn in late autumn 1977, the destroyer navigated its way to the Pacific whereupon it set course for Victoria, British Columbia, Canada. While underway, regulars trained reservists in navigation, helmsmanship, communication, ship safety, and seamanship. Upon reaching Victoria, British Columbia, its crew enjoyed a weeklong stay of activities before returning to Portland.

By mid-1978, *Hamner* was underway for training exercises. Having transited the river, she set course for San Diego where she picked up reservists at the Thirty-Second Street Naval Station, for two weeks of training. While there, her crew looked in amazement at the navy's newest DDs and FFGs with just two ribbons on their bridge wing, and then with great pride, observed *Hamner's* service ribbons Battle E, OPS E, COMM C, and the

Engineering E paint on the forward stack, reminding them of the combat experience of the old destroyer they were proud to be manning. Steaming to Hawaii, the *Hamner* trained with aircraft carriers involving plane guard and conducted anti-submarine warfare exercises. Here, the crew found Honolulu liberty a dream come true before returning to the States.

As a Navy Reserve Force-Pacific (NRF-P) training vessel, *Hamner* served as a training platform for naval reservists. Manning was always an issue since her crew complement was 60 percent regulars and 40 percent reservists, and many times, in order to get underway, *cross-decking (transferring)* sailors from other destroyers became necessary. *Some* of *Hamner's* cruises were undertaken without any reservists aboard, making it difficult for the smaller-crew to keep the ship working at full capacity.

By late 1978, having once again left the slough at Swan Island with her crew "manning the rails" in their petty officer coats, *Hamner* again slid quietly beneath St. John's Bridge on the Willamette River, wending her way toward the mouth of the Columbia River as new reservists watched the lights of Portland fade. They felt the thrill of adventure in being an American naval sailor. When reaching Astoria and unable to transit the shoal sand bar due to weather conditions, the destroyer would moor at the Thunderbird Motel pier where

Hamner conducted drills in General Quarters, damage control and man overboard exercises. These drills were the same as those conducted when at sea. While there, her regular crew maintained the normal in-port duty section watches, leaving the reservists to have liberty in the event they chose to go ashore.

On the destroyer weekend training would be conducted as she passed through the Desdemona Shoal and entered the Pacific, waves splashing at her bridge.

"Bridge, radio room."

"Radio room, aye."

"Captain, sir, it is going to be a rough day at sea. Sir, with your permission, may I pipe to the bridge my favorite song by Simon & Garfunkel?"

"Proceed, radioman."

"Aye, aye, Captain."

The bridge crew sang aloud, "Homeward bound, I wish I was homeward bound, home where my thoughts escape me, home where my music is playing, home where my love life lies waiting silently for me, silently for me, oh, homeward bound, oh. I wish I was homeward bound." As the destroyer pitched and rolled and her crew sang, making the best of their watch, how little did they know it was her last voyage at sea. By weekend, *Hamner* was homeward bound for Portland, never again to sail the river or the ocean she knew so well.

Wending beneath the Broadway Bridge, Steel Bridge, Burnside Bridge, Morrison Bridge, and the Hawthorne Bridge, as June in the summer of 1979 rolled in, the *Hamner*, her end as a US Navy destroyer, made her last voyage with a skeleton crew, accompanied by the other destroyer at Portland, the USS *John Roger*, some two miles up the Willamette River from the reserve center to attend the annual Portland Rose Festival. With a fresh coat of paint covering her aging hull, and her fore and aft lines tied to cleats mounted on the river quay wall, *Hamner's* crew, to their delight, danced in the streets to live music until the wee hours of the morning and drank as guests of the city until the festival's end. As one young crewman put it, "Wow! Where have these lumberjack girls been keeping themselves?"

U.S.S. HAMNER (DD-718)
FLEET POST OFFICE
SAN FRANCISCO, CALIFORNIA 96601

FOR IMMEDIATE RELEASE. . . . . MARCH 6, 1979.

The Portland based destroyer, USS HAMNER (DD-718) has taken top honors in the annual Battle Efficiency Competition Awards. Presented by the Commander-in-Chief of the U.S. Pacific Fleet, the Battle Efficiency "E" has been awarded to the officers and crew of USS HAMNER for superior levels of readiness and training during 1978. HAMNER's crew also won special awards in Gunnery, Engineering and Communications. USS ROGERS (DD-876), also homeported in Portland, was runner-up in the Battle Efficiency Competition. The Portland based ships won the awards over other destroyers stationed in Tacoma and Seattle.

USS ROGERS was commissioned in 1945 and USS HAMNER in 1946. Both ships saw action in Korea and Vietnam. HAMNER and ROGERS are responsible for training Selected Reservists in the local Oregon and southern Washington area. Over 180 regular Navy, active-duty officers and men man each ship. The ships are units of Destroyer Squadron THIRTY-SEVEN. USS HAMNER is commanded by Commander J. E. WHITELY, Jr., of Coronado California. USS ROGERS is commanded by Commander C. J. THOMAS of Portland. Both ships are scheduled for decommissioning in fiscal year 1980.

Point of contact for further information: LTJG Rick Anderson
USS HAMNER (DD-718)
Telephone (good through 30 MAR)
AC (714) 235-1211

# # # #

Press Release—Battle Efficiency Competition Award

Rick Anderson

Marc McConahy 1977-78

Frank Fannick 1975-78

Sid Johnson

Carl Martin (far left) 1977-79

Columbia River Bar Pilot Boat

USS Ranger (CVA-CV-61)

Refueling USS Hamner from USS Ranger (above)
Crew (L-R) Sword, Bender, Reimann, Thomas

Chapter 15

Attention on Deck—Strike the Pennant, 1979

By the late 1970s, the *Hamner's* future was becoming clear, as the Department of the Navy issued directives that all remaining Gearing-class destroyers were to be decommissioned and either sold to a foreign entity or scrapped by the decade's end. After thirty-four years of service to her country, the demise and fate of the *Hamner* had been sealed. At that time, a new class of destroyers (Spruance) was rapidly replacing the Gearing class.

On October 1, 1979, the USS *Hamner* (DD-718) was decommissioned at the Center in Portland, with the ceremonies she deserved. She was and remains the pride of her crews, the United States Navy, and of this nation. After the decommissioning of the *Hamner*, the foreign government of Taiwan showed an interest in procuring her. However, with the recognition of the People's Republic of China, the laws of the United States would not permit the Department of the Navy to sell her directly to Taiwan.

Hamner was eventually sold to a Taiwanese scrap metal company, which had towed her to Taiwan and in turn sold her to Taiwan on December 17, 1980. She was renamed as guided missile destroyer *Yun Yang* (DDG-927). She continued to be operational until the *Yun Yang* (DD-927) was decommissioned on December 16, 2003. *Hamner* was sunk by *Hai Hu* (SS-794) as a target exercise off Pingtung, Taiwan, on September 6, 2005. The ship's final resting place is on the floor of the South China Sea, through which she had passed so many times in her long service with the US Navy.

By late 1980, the last of the Gearing-class destroyers at the Naval and Marine Corps Center had either been scrapped or sold to a foreign country.

The *Hamner* as we knew her is now gone. Today, her ship's bell stands guard at the entrance to the United States Naval Hospital, Camp Pendleton, Oceanside, California. The plaque and bell were dedicated on December 1, 1982, "In Honor of All Who Hear the Call of Navy Medicine."

In 1992, the USS *Hamner* (DD-718) Association was formed at Farragut State Park, Idaho, during their first reunion since the sailors served on the *Hamner*.

With the passage of time, many of the *Hamner's* former crew have remained close to each other. Many have become buddies for life, and even when former crew members pass away, their wives still have lunch together, keeping in touch when they can and attending reunions when possible.

When you sail the sometimes-hostile waters of the Pacific or the Columbia River often with fellow crew members and risk your lives together, through it all you develop friendships for life. The association continues to work towards keeping the memories alive and well for her shipmates, their families, and those interested in this beautiful lady.

Today, although *Hamner* is no longer with us, memory of her remains, reminding us of not only a vanished class of ships but also a vanished way of life.

Hamner served the United States Navy for thirty-four years and then the Taiwanese Navy for another twenty-three years. Crews from both countries still follow her and honor her with stories and photographs. I have told the story of a destroyer named *Hamner*, the times she knew, and the crewmen who knew her. The story reflects times of peace and war, pleasure and peril, and tales of her crew. I have told the story of a vessel, from the time of commission to the time of decommissioning, a story of an amazing warship of the United States Navy.

To the officers and men of the *Hamner* who contributed their valiant shares to our Navy traditions, I drink a deep-sea toast. To those men and women and their ships to come, who will carry on and create new traditions, I give the time-honored hail and farewell:

"Fair winds and following seas."

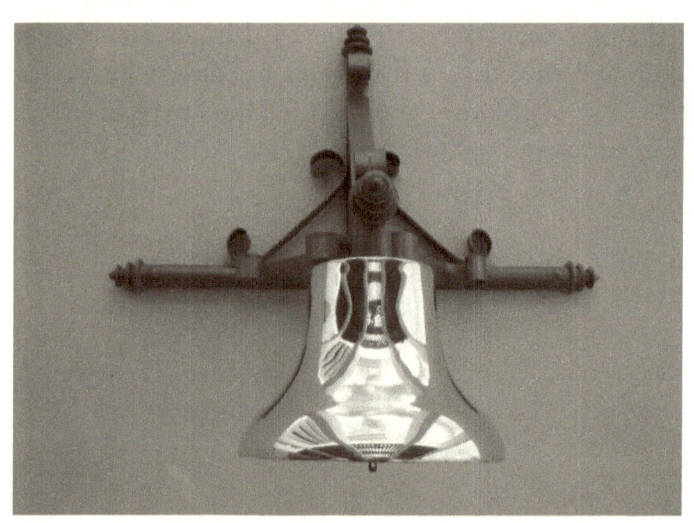

USS Hamner (DD-718) Ship's Bell

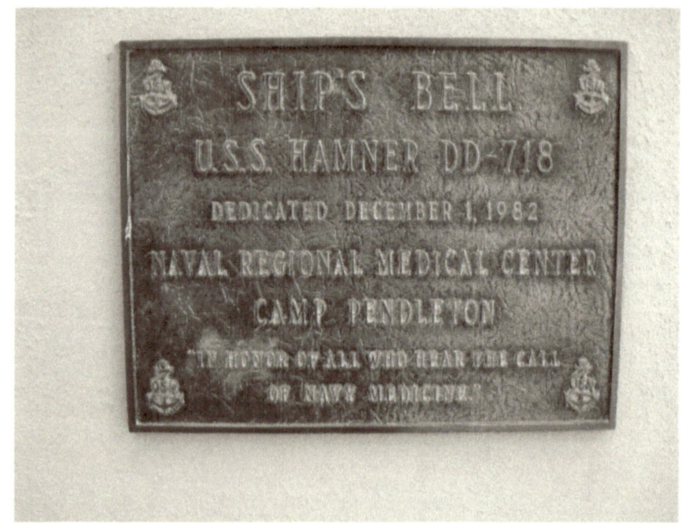

Clyde Jenson, Founder at 1992 Reunion

The Many Generations of Hamner
Patches and a Pewter Plaque

Showing the shipmates' pride in their ship

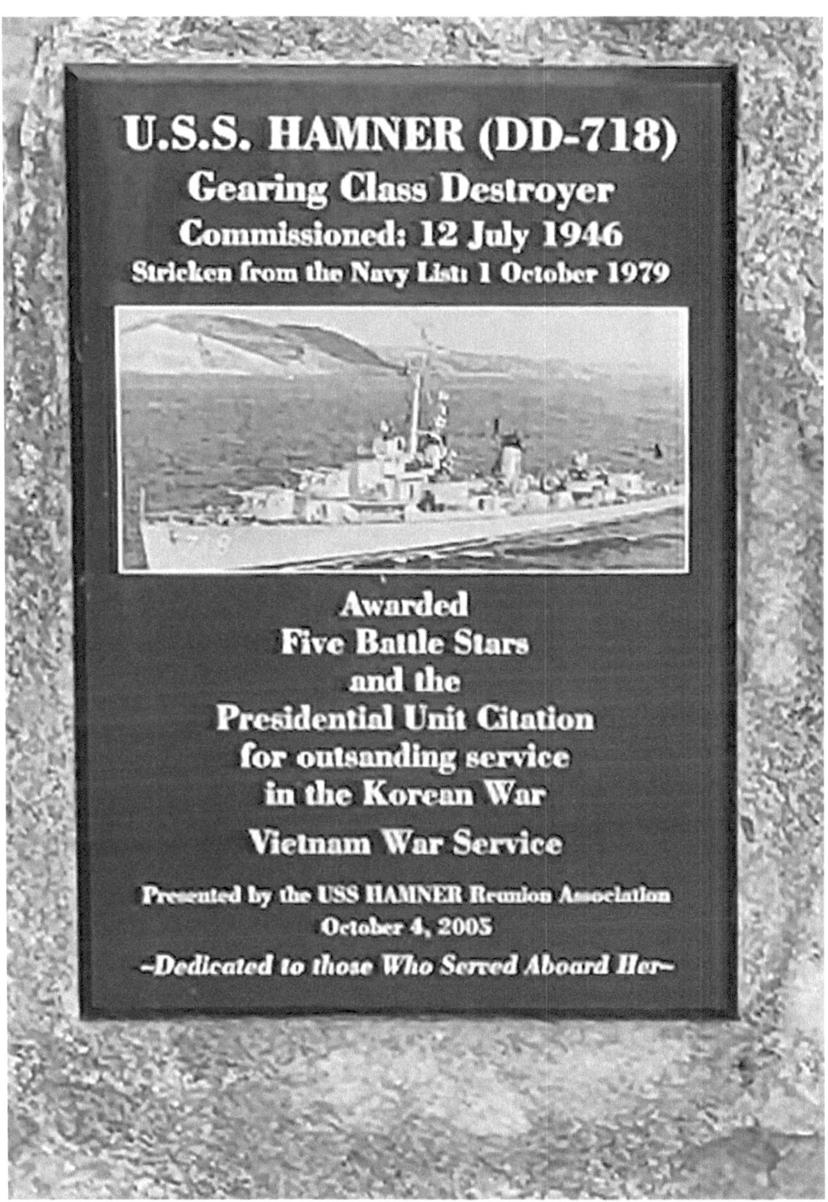

Plaque placed by the Association during the 2005 reunion at the
National Museum of the Pacific War in Fredericksburg, Texas

This plaque was sponsored by the Association in 2015 and is now a part of the Mt. Soledad National Veterans Memorial in San Diego, CA

APPENDIX 1

---⊙---

A Sailor's Reflections on the Versatility of the Modern Destroyer

I believe this story of the operations of the *Hamner* during the Korean conflict from July 25, 1950, when she left a Japanese base for Taiwan, until October 31, 1950, when the tempo of naval war had slowed in Korea, is the story of the modern destroyer's place in naval warfare. The *Hamner* operated in three areas—distinct, geographically, and tactically. The Taiwan patrol was the first, the blockade and bombardment of the east coast of Korea the second, and the carrier operations off Inchon and Wonsan were the third.

During the week after the president announced his decision to intervene in Korea, the *Hamner* took on the additional supplies and ammunition necessary to fight a war. After one of the fastest trips made by a destroyer across the Pacific, she arrived in Sasebo, which was to be her base for the remainder of the conflict. On the way across the Pacific, the *Hamner* joined the three other destroyers and the cruiser with whom she was to operate as a task group for six weeks. On July 26 the task group left Sasebo early in the morning for the first wartime cruise of the *Hamner*.

The ships headed toward Korea for most of the day until orders sent them southward toward the other danger spot—Taiwan. The task group steamed up and down the Taiwan Strait in a formation which would give the greatest swept area consistent with the protection of the cruiser. The watch on the radar scopes and the lookouts on the bridge were on the alert constantly, watching for any ships since the purpose of the task group was to help prevent any landing on Taiwan by the Communist Chinese and to stop any invasion of the mainland originating in Taiwan. When contact was sighted and was at all suspicious, the destroyer nearest it would leave the formation and investigate. Although the *Hamner* investigated several contacts each day, all of them proved to be merchant men who were carrying on normal trade. After a week, the task group was ordered back to Sasebo.

The second phase of the *Hamner's* operations began shortly afterward when she steamed out of Sasebo Harbor in the company of the task group. They were bound for Korea, and this time the ships steamed up the east coast to Tanchon where they were to bombard marshaling yards south of the city. Also the ships would fire on any *targets of opportunity* that presented themselves. The bombardment was successful with many hits observed on the yards and on the tracks. Several of the destroyers took part in the actual bombardment while the *Hamner* laid off to the seaward, a part of the anti-submarine screen for the other ships.

The next day, the task group steamed south and bombarded bridges and the highway that clung to the hills which rose from the sea. The traffic along the highway was the target of the *Hamner* for the next several days. The ship would lie off the beach without a light showing and wait for the lights of the enemy trucks coming around a turn in the road. When several trucks had rounded the turn, the ship's guns opened up in a roaring salvo. The projectiles screamed into the midst of the trucks, exploding in blinding, deadly flashes. The trucks and their lights disappeared. The *Hamner* moved along the coast a short distance and repeated the deadly performance.

During the day, when the trucks did not move, the *Hamner*, with one or two of the other destroyers, made shipping sweeps up and down the coast watching for blockade runners. The North Korean Navy consisted of small craft, mostly minesweepers and mine layers in addition to a few patrol craft. However, the enemy often seized sampans, tugs, and junks to land its troops behind the United Nations' lines. The destroyers were out to stop such traffic. One morning while on the blockade sweep, the *Hamner* contacted two junks pulling three sampans apiece. The craft did not stop when they saw the destroyers bearing down on them. Instead, the small craft was made for the beach. The guns of the *Hamner* swung into position and with precision fire battered the craft into driftwood.

Even though the *Hamner* and other ships were cutting the enemy's supply lines on the east coast, he still had enough supplies at the front to mount continuing pressure on the South Korean forces. At Yongdok he had the South Koreans pushed into a pocket with their backs to the sea. But instead of the sea being a barrier, the task group made it an exit. The destroyers, with the cooperation of the shore fire control party, pounded the enemy positions with deadly accuracy during the day and night. Then the destroyers made preparations to take the South Koreans off the beach in the destroyers' boats. The enemy was to be kept away from the beach by keeping a steady rain of harassing and interdiction fire falling on his positions. The destroyers did not have to use their boats because two LSTs showed up in time to snatch the South Koreans out of the trap, while the destroyers increased the tempo of the bombardment to hold the enemy pinned down and ineffectual.

The destroyers escorted the LSTs southward to a point still in possession of the United Nations where the South Koreans were put ashore to continue their battle against the communists. The task group continued south, to return to port to replenish and to enjoy a little liberty. When they sortied again, they headed for their old stomping grounds. However, this time the ships kept going farther and farther north, continually searching for blockade runners. No traffic was seen on the sea nor along the highway which the ships had bombarded on the previous mission. The task group continued northward until the men wondered if the admiral were heading for Russia.

Just short of the border, the task group turned, and the commander led the ships into a bay to the target, the city of Chongjin. A helicopter was launched to reconnoiter, and, after he had given the city a close search, the bombardment was called off because there were no targets in the area. On the way south, the other destroyers and the cruiser fired on railroad bridges and a line of box cars. The *Hamner* stayed to the seaward in the anti-submarine screen. In addition to the anti-submarine search, the *Hamner* was from time to time sent to investigate small craft that had been picked up visually or by radar. All of these proved to be Korean patrol vessels.

The task group steamed south to Pohang where the ROK troops were falling back slowly under heavy pressure from the Communists. During the first day, while the other destroyers were in shore bombardment stations, the pressure slackened. The destroyers fired only harassing and interdiction fire on the enemy lines. When the *Hamner* moved into position to relieve the other destroyers, she started the same routine. One mount fired a few rounds every hour at each of ten to twenty targets, whose coordinates had been furnished by the shore fire patrol party operating with the ROK forces ashore.

The communists, however, were realizing that the war was being prolonged beyond their capacity to win unless they made good a thrust through Pohang to Pusan. That night the enemy's push began. The shore party saw concentrations of troops forming in front of the ROK lines. By radio, the spotters sent the position of these concentrations to the *Hamner* with the request for rapid fire. The twin guns of the *Hamner* burst forth again and again with a bright flash that lighted the ship and sent projectiles whining toward the targets. As combat correlated the information and sent it to the plotting room, the guns shifted from one concentration to another. The strangely distorted voices of the spotters often included in their firing orders words of praise—"Well done. Beautiful shooting. It is landing right in the middle of them."

As the day broke over the sea, the *Hamner* shifted to harassing fire she had started the evening before. The communists were still in the same positions, but the heavy artillery of the *Hamner* had beaten off the attack. During the day, the other destroyers took up the shore bombardment.

The night watch of the *Hamner* caught a little rest while the men on duty patrolled the harbor entrance on the alert lookout for enemy craft who might try to attack the ships bombarding. In the early afternoon, the ship was ordered to Pusan to fuel. After a fast trip down, the *Hamner* fueled in the harbor while the crew looked the town over—through long glasses. The trip back to the task group was at a slower speed. The remainder of the night was spent patrolling.

Early in the morning, the ship again moved in to relieve another destroyer at the shore bombardment station. The *Hamner* started the day firing harassing and interdiction fire. The situation on land had changed since the *Hamner* had last fired. The interruptions to the harassing fire were not to bring rapid fire to bear on some concentrations building up for an offensive—the targets were defensive positions that had to be broken up before the push could start.

Then came what the men of the *Hamner* had worked for—a call for blanket fire on an area. After ten minutes of pounding, the shore party ordered "Cease fire. The front line is moving forward, and its exact position is in doubt." The *Hamner* was relieved before the lines became settled again.

Pohang was the last offensive operation in which the *Hamner* took part in this stage of the war. When she steamed from her firing station that day, she steamed into another part of the conflict—into a different area, with a different fleet, and into an entirely different role. She became one of the screens for the carriers in the famous Task Force 77. As one of the screens, the *Hamner* was never mentioned in news dispatches or naval histories that focused on the carrier operations in the war. However, the screening destroyers are a very important part of the task force. The destroyers work hard to keep their stations on the screen. They have to work hard because the thirty knots that the carriers make with ease in launching or recovering flight operations are hard on the destroyers' engines, hard on her hull, and hard on her men. The destroyers turn, reorient, and rush to the plane guard station as the carriers search for favorable winds across their flight decks to launch and recover their aircraft. The whole point of this frantic movement on the part of the destroyers is to provide an effective shield for the carriers against enemy air, surface, and submarine attacks.

The pilots of the carriers' planes feel reassured when, during night operations, several of the destroyers move into positions ahead of the carrier or almost in her wake to be near if any pilot is forced to land his craft in the water. Not only near at hand do the destroyers guard for fallen aviators. The *Hamner* also left the main body of the task force for two-day periods and operated on a distant station. This station was in an area over which aircraft, returning from strikes, were likely to pass and where the disabled may ditch, and the pilots be picked up immediately.

Another duty performed many times by the *Hamner* was the transfer of mail and freight between ships within the task force. The administration of the many ships of a carrier task force results in more communications and reports than can be effectively handled by the radio and visual communication channels. The destroyers are called on to pass this *guard mail* between the carriers, the cruisers, and other destroyers. In addition, since not all of the task force fuels at any onetime, light freight, mail, and passengers are first transferred from the tankers to the destroyers. The destroyers carry this *cargo* to its ultimate destination and transfer it when they rejoin the task force.

The operations with the carriers were entirely different from the patrols and bombarding of the east coast of Korea, but the men of the *Hamner* knew that, even though the carriers got most of the recognition and "the glory" arising from the operations of the aircraft attached to the carriers, the carriers can never safely operate without the *small boys* along to protect them and to deliver their light freight.

Robert O'Malley
SKC 1948–1951
USS *Hamner* (DD-718)

Appendix 2

◉

An Ensign's Song—
Farewell Alameda

*Farewell song from the USS Hamner (DD-718) to ALAMEDA
upon departure from Task Force 77.*

"Farewell, Alameda"
(To the tune of Alouette)

Alameda,
All praise to Alameda
Alameda
Our dear OTC
When there's nothing else to do
Speed of thirty knots will do
It's all right
While we fight
But there'll be no bath tonight
Oh—oh—oh—oh

Alameda,
We sing to Alameda
Alameda
All hail authority

When everyone is in a fog
Then we hear, "Affirm Mike Dog" (*spoken*)
Never fear
While you're here
There's no danger when he's near
Oh—oh—oh—oh

Alameda,
A cheer for Alameda—(Hooray!)
Alameda
Pourquoi, je ne sais[12]
When we've settled for the night
Rings a voice so clear and bright
You're the one
Start to run
"Fishmarket, take plane guard number *one*!" (*spoken*)
Oh—oh—oh—oh (*Ouch*)

Alameda,
Goodbye, Alameda
Alameda
Alas we say adieu
Eight long months a screen tin can
"Rotate station; fill the van"
We hate to leave
You see us grieve
"Pardon boys, I think I'll heave" (*spoken*)

We think it's great
On any date
To pass mail and light freight
Jammed together
In a closet
A degree too much, you'll get a posit

---

[12] Translation: why, I do not know

To each call
You're the ball
As Dickens said, "God bless us all!" (*spoken*)

Now we're done
Our rest begun
California here we come (to the tune)

Oh—oh—oh—oh

Alameda,
Farewell, Alameda
Alameda
"This is fishmarket, how do you hear me, over?"
(*spoken*)

Lyrics by: Ensign James D. Hutchinson
USS *Hamner* (DD-718)
Friday, March 9, 1951

APPENDIX 3

US Navy Reserves (USNR)—A History

Reservists aboard *Hamner* came from many walks of life. Some had previously served aboard American man-of-war vessels, while others were newly enlisted sailors. When asked why they signed up for the reserve, most stated they never intended to make the navy a career, but knew their work and training aboard *Hamner* was important, and they were going to do the very best they could. With *Hamner* now assigned to the Navy Reserve Force, it is worth noting, how the USNR came to be.

The United States Navy Reserve (USNR) was known as the US Naval Reserve from 1915–2005. The USNR's roots go far back in our nation's history. Back to the "state navies" of the Revolutionary War, and although these forces were disbanded after the war was over, the idea of a naval militia run by individual states had been firmly implanted in our new nation. When the states failed to reestablish their militias, President Thomas Jefferson proposed setting up a national naval militia. Congress, however, wouldn't vote the necessary money to implement the President's plan.

The lack of a trained pool of men from which to bolster naval forces in time of war continued to be a problem until shortly after the start of the Civil War, when because of a lack of skilled seamen, Union ships laid unmanned. Congress quickly moved to alleviate this naval shortage and passed an act on July 24, 1861, that authorized the hiring of ships and crew for "the temporary increase of the Navy." Eventually, more than half of the Union fleet consisted of "reserve ships" (merchant vessels, tugs, yachts, and ferries) which became known as "Abe Lincoln's soapbox navy." The force grew from ninety ships to seven hundred, with nearly fifty-eight thousand sailors, nearly all of them volunteers.

When the Civil War ended, the ships and men were released. The idea of maintaining a permanent reserve of citizen sailors still hadn't taken hold.

The next attempt to form a navy reserve was made in 1879 when a group of former naval officers gathered in New York to make plans for a Reserve Corps. Their recommendations, however, were never acted upon, and by 1883, public support in the nation for even the active regular navy was negligible.

The modern navy reserve movement began in 1887 when the United States had come to the end of its continental expansion. On February 17, a bill was introduced in Congress that would create a naval reserve of auxiliary cruisers, officers, and men from the mercantile marines of the United States. It didn't become law, but the Navy Department set up a plan for a state navy militia force. Massachusetts became the first state to create a militia the following year, and many states followed suit in the years to come. These militia were organized on a local basis, and former ex-navy men regularly drilled and made occasional cruises.

Early in January 1893, the Navy assigned the old battleship USS *New Hampshire* to the state of New York for use by its naval militia, and in August, Congress passed an act that authorized the temporary loan of vessels to the states for training purposes. In most cases, regular navy personnel were assigned to the ships.

By 1914, after years of congressional debate, the Naval Militia Act was passed into law, placing the naval militia under the Navy Department, making it possible in time of war to bring the militia into federal service. And by 1915, Congress approved the "authority for a United States Naval Reserve to consist of citizens" of the United States who have been or may be entitled to be honorably discharged from the Navy. There were, however, no provisions in the law for pay or for any type of drills or training, except that members might be required to perform one to two months' active service aboard fleet ships each year.

There was little incentive for anyone to sign up for this kind of service, so finally in 1915, a new Naval Reserve Force Act was passed by Congress that authorized pay and uniforms for the citizen sailors, and established a training program for them. It opened membership in the Naval Reserve Force to any civilian who had sea experience, whether or not he had ever served in the regular navy.

During this time, President Woodrow Wilson was trying to keep the United States out of the war in Europe; however, by 1917, Germany had threatened the United States with unrestricted submarine warfare to sink ships in the Atlantic ocean, although they offered to spare American ships if they carried no ammunitions and notified the Germans when they were sailing and what routes they were taking. This seemed like an ultimatum. Would the United States need permission before sending any ship into the Atlantic? In response to this threat and other provocation (April 6, 1917), the United States felt compelled to declare war on Germany.

The US Navy, along with its newly organized Naval Reserve Force, geared itself for action, knowing it was going to take a lot of manpower to fight this war. At the time, one of the worst shortages in the Navy was clerical help: secretaries, file clerks, typists, and personnel with all the skills needed to handle the vastly increased paperwork of an expanding navy during wartime.

To remedy the problem, the secretary of the navy had an idea. He asked his legal experts if there was any reason why a yeoman (the name of the rating given sailors specializing in clerical work) had to be a man. He was advised that the law did not specifically state that yeomen had to be male, so the secretary promptly suggested that women be allowed to join the Naval Reserve Force as yeomen.

The response of patriotic, dedicated women was immediate. Thousands of them flocked to the recruiting stations and took the oath as naval reservists. They soon became known as "yeomanettes" or "yeowomen." From this early and difficult start, the modern United States Navy Reserves we know today has evolved, and *Hamner* was part of it.

APPENDIX 4

Deck Log Poetry

In the night we hear a bell
It's midnight on the old *Bausell*

Sixty-one is no more
It's been mustered out the door

Despite the extensions by JFK
It didn't last even one more day

Bausell is moored to berth 63
Hamner is the outboard of four DDs

Anderson and *Agerholmn* are in between
Rounding out the peaceful scene

Standard mooring lines are double
No wires out 'cause there'll be no trouble

We're at the place that we like most
NAVSTA, San Diego, is our New Year's host

Around the harbor you will meet
Ships of the US Pacific Fleet

Ships of friendly nations too
Are greeting 1962

On North Island, in his air dale shack
Is the SOPA, COMNAVAIRPAC

The bachelors tonight are out in the town
Burning all their bridges down

For tomorrow, this tired old tin can
Will head for Frisco and a Mark I FRAM

Arnold J. Case LTJG, USNR
USS *Hamner* (DD-718)
Monday, January 1, 1962
00-04 San Diego, California

APPENDIX 5

USS Hamner (DD-718)
Association

Established 1992

Our association was started in August 1992 when approximately sixty-five shipmates and family members met in Idaho for our first reunion. That was over thirty years ago, and we are still spreading the word. We are a nonprofit veterans group with a mission to preserve the memories of this great ship and her crews. In this book, written by one of our own (Ken Ericksen) and edited by an association officer (with the help of many shipmates), the story of the *Hamner* will be shared outside our *official* group, and we hope this is just the beginning. Our website is a growing repository of photographs, cruise books, reunion books, and memorial pages. As we acquire documents, memorabilia, and photographs, we continue to add to that repository, and we will continue to do so. The association also has a ship store where you can purchase items to show your pride in the *Hamner*. We do not sell these items for profit unless the selling is labeled as a fund raiser; they are sold to help us keep the memories alive.

All are welcome to join us, attend our reunions, and help us spread the word. Our contact information is listed below. Please help us find more *Hamner* shipmates and families so we can continue the story of the USS *Hamner*.

Contact Information for the USS *Hamner* (DD-718) Association:
- www.hamnerdd718.squarespace.com
- https://business.facebook.com/HamnerDD718
- hamnerdd718@gmail.com

Glossary of Naval Acronyms

AD. Destroyer tender

AE. Ammunition ship

AN/WQC-2 (or UQC). Underwater telephone used on manned submersibles and many Navy surface ships. Voice or morse code communicated through the UQC are altered to a high pitch for transmission through water.

AO. Oiler

ARG. Amphibious ready group which contains US Navy warships, known as an ATF

ASROC. Anti-submarine rocket

ASW. Anti-submarine warfare

ATF. Amphibious task force

BB. Battleship

CA. Heavy cruiser

CHOP. Change operational command: *out-chop* would mean the ship is heading *home*

CIC. Combat information center

CL. Light cruiser

CV. Aircraft carrier

CVA. Large attack aircraft carrier

CVL. Small aircraft carrier

DASH. Drone anti-submarine helicopter

DD. Destroyer

DDG. Guided missile destroyer

DDR. Radar picket destroyer

DE. Destroyer escort

DesDiv. Destroyer division

DesRon. Destroyer squadron

DMZ. Demilitarized zone

ECM. Electronic counter measure

FF. Frigate

FFG. Guided missile frigate (the last one decommissioned in 2015)

FRAM. Fleet rehabilitation and modernization

H&I fire. 1. Harassment and interdiction fire—a type of artillery mission used by the US during both world wars and Korea and Vietnam wars, such as periodic firing of rounds at trails or transports known to be used by the enemy

LCM. Landing craft mechanized

LSI. Landing ship, infantry

LST. Landing ship, tank

MiG. A soviet fighter aircraft named for the founders of the design bureau Mikoyan (M) and(i) Gurevich (G)

NGFS. Naval gunfire support of troops fighting o land

OOD. Officer of the deckn

PBY (flying boats). The Consolidated PBY Catalina is a flying boat and amphibious aircraft that was produced in the 1930s and 1940s, used primarily for long range and search and rescue at sea. The PBY designatio: *PB* means patrol bomber, and *Y* was the code assigned to the original manufacturer, Consolidated Aircraft.

PIRAZ. Positive identification RADAR advisory zone

PPI. Plan position indicator which is a type of radar display. The radar antenna is in the center of the display and the distance from the antenna and the distance above the ground are drawn in circles.

ROK. Republic of Korea

SAR. Search and rescue

SLR-2. Shipboard ECM receiver (antenna used with electronic countermeasures)

TF and TG. Task force and task group

WestPac. Western Pacific

GLOSSARY

aft. Rear of the ship

anchor's aweigh. When the anchor has just cleared the bottom and the ship starts to move forward

Battle "E". Battle Efficiency Award (now the Battle Effectiveness Award) is awarded every year to a small number of US Navy ships that win their battle effectiveness/efficiency competition. The award is specially painted on the ship.

bridge. Raised area or platform where the ship is conned and steered, usually in the forward of the ship

bow. Forward (front) part of a ship

buttoned up. A secured measure for the safety of the ship and crew who were not allowed topside

Condition Zebra. Condition Zebra is set during General Quarters, ship-wide casualties, when entering and leaving a port during wartime, or anytime the ship is in danger against fire, flooding, and other damage. All doors labeled with a black X, black Y, or red Z remain closed.

conn. To direct helmsmen on how to move the rudder and control the engines

deck. Equivalent to floors in a building

destroyer. A small warship designed to escort, help, and defend larger capital ships, such as aircraft carriers, battleships, and cruisers, or to conduct independent operations, often in groups such as reconnaissance, naval gunfire support (of troops on land), or anti-submarine warfare.

destroyer tender. A destroyer tender is a type of depot or auxiliary ship used to provide maintenance support to a flotilla of destroyers or other small warships.

dixie cup. White cap worn by enlisted sailors

ensign. 1. The word ensign is applied to the flag flown at the stern by naval vessels in commission or by merchant vessels. The U.S. Navy's ensign is the same as the national flag, but other navies may have distinctive naval ensigns for their vessels.
2. US Navy—lowest rank of a commissioned officer

fleet. Organization of ships and aircraft under the command of one commander; can include all types of ships and aircraft needed.

forward. Front part of the ship; toward the bow

General Quarters. Condition of readiness when naval action is imminent; all battle stations fully manned and alert; ammunition is ready to load; guns and guided missile launchers may be loaded.

greyhound. Term used for a swift ship, sometimes used to describe fast warships

helm. Tiller, or rudder and gear that turn the tiller

helmsman. The man who steers the ship

hunter killer. Prolonged operations conducted in specific situations by a specifically organized force

kamikaze. 1. Divine wind to protect the homeland (Japanese meaning) 2. part of the special attack units of Japan; pilots flew suicide attacks against allied naval vessels beginning on October 25, 1944.

leave. Authorized time off the ship (absence) of more than forty-eight hours

lee helmsman. The man who controls the ship's engines and speed

liberty. Authorized time off the ship of less than forty-eight hours

motor whaleboat. A power boat pointed at both ends; usually twenty-six feet.

nest. Two or more ships moored alongside each other

out-chop. chop means "change operational command" as in to change from one operating area to another (i.e.: a ship in the

7th Fleet heading home to the 3rd Fleet would out-chop when crossing line drawn on a chart to show operating areas)

picket boat. A picket boat is a small naval craft used for harbor patrol and are often carried as a ship's boat. They can be between thirty-three and fifty-five feet.

pilot. An expert in local waters who comes aboard to help the captain navigate the ship; pilot advises the captain on how the ship should be controlled.

plane guard. A warship (usually a destroyer or frigate but sometimes an aircraft like a helicopter) which is responsible for recovering the aircrew of planes or helicopters which crash (ditch) in the ocean.

plank owner. Anyone serving on the ship at the time of commissioning; certificates usually presented to these shipmates.

pollywog. A young sailor who has never crossed the equator and therefore has not been initiated by Neptunus Rex and his shellbacks

port. Left side of the ship facing forward

salvo. A simultaneous firing of artillery and/or guns in battle

sampan. Small traditional boats used in the harbors and rivers of China and Japan; they usually have a sail and an awning. They can also be rowed from the stern.

shellback. An old or veteran sailor who has crossed the equator and been initiated by Neptunus Rex during the ceremony (former pollywog)

shifting colors. Changing from one flag display to another; the desired effect is one set of flags vanishing and another flashing out at the same time. Ships take pride in achieving this effect. Bluejacket's Manual: "A ship that does not shift colors smartly will soon have a reputation she does not want."

skunk. Contact surface on water, often by radar detection

starboard. Right side of the ship—looking forward

star shell. A form of artillery used to illuminate the battlefield at night and also a way of passing signals. When fired, the shell bursts while at a certain height—a flare burns, and then the parachute in the shell slows its falling.

stern. rear (aftermost part) of the ship (on which the fantail sits)

task force or group. A task force (TF) is divided into task groups (TG). Task groups are assigned numbers corresponding to the particular task force of which they are a part. For instance, TF 77 may have a task group assigned to reconnaissance, and its designated number could be TG 77.3.

Viet Cong. "Viet Nam Cong San," the communist revolutionary group in South Vietnam, Laos, and Cambodia which fought against the government of South Vietnam whose capital was Saigon, and its ally the United States

wending. Going in a specific direction, usually slowly or indirectly

Yankee Station. This was a location off the coast of North Vietnam where US Navy aircraft carriers and other task force vessels would remain in the open waters to provide support by launching air strikes against enemy targets.

BIBLIOGRAPHY

Only the sources and writings that were used in the editing of this book are listed. This is not a complete list of all the resources consulted. These sources have enabled editing decisions, enhanced the writing, and minimized errors. For those who want to consult more naval history, this list is a good place to start.

Bureau of Naval Personnel. *Seaman*. Washington, DC. Government Printing Office. 1952.

Field, James A. Jr. *History of United States Naval Operations, Korea.* Washington, DC: U.S. Government Printing Office. 1962.

Grant, George, Angus Konstam, Leo Marriott. *From the Galley to the Present Day. Warships.* New York: Gramercy Books/PRC Publishing. 2001.

Karnow, Stanley. *Vietnam, a History.* New York: The Viking Press. 1983.

Kaplan, Philip. *FLY NAVY Naval Aviators and Carrier Aviation—A History. London: Metro Books.* Aurum Press Ltd. 2001.

Mack, Vice Adm William P. Mack, USN (ret.), Capt. Harry A. Seymour Jr, USN (ret), and CDR. Lesa A. McComas, USN. *The Naval Officer's Guide.* Maryland: Naval Institute Press. 1998.

Miller, Nathan. *The Naval Air War 1939–1945.* Maryland: Naval Institute Press. 1991.

Noel, Captain John V. Jr. U.S. Navy and Master Chief Journalist William J. Miller U.S. Navy (ret.). *The Bluejackets' Manual Seventeenth Edition.* Maryland: U.S. Naval Institute. 1967.

Palmer, Norman. *The Naval Institute Guide to the Ships and Aircraft of the U.S. Fleet.* Maryland: Naval Institute Press, 1997 (Sixteenth Edition).

Prange, Gordon W. with Donald M. Goldstein and Katharine V. Dillon. *Miracle at Midway.* New York: Penguin Books by arrangement with McGraw-Hill Book Company. 1983.

Sumrall, Robert F. *Sumner-Gearing—Class Destroyers.* Maryland: Naval Institute Press. 1995.

Thus evermore shall rise to Thee,
Glad hymns of praise
from land and sea.

About the Editor

Patty Hathaway

Patty Hathaway has always loved veterans, the US Navy, and the sea. She has served the American Legion and Auxiliary for many years and has been an officer of the USS *Hamner* DD-718 Association for thirteen years, dedicated to preserving the memory of the ship and her crews. Patty also uses her skills as a professional photographer to preserve photographs, books, and other documents for the association. Patty is married to Merrill Hathaway, a line officer aboard the *Hamner* during the Vietnam War, enjoys ocean cruising, and is proud to have retraced the *Hamner*'s wake during a month-long crossing of the Pacific Ocean as a part of the *Pacific Princess'* world cruise in 2018. Patty lives with her husband, Merrill, and their Kerry Blue Terrier, Brandon, in Maryland not far from the US Naval Academy, the Chesapeake Bay, and the Atlantic Ocean.

Brandon Hathaway SN
(The Unofficial Mascot of the Association)

About the Author

Ken Ericksen

Ken Ericksen served as an enlisted man in the United States Navy from 1952 to 1956. After serving in the Aleutian Islands, he was transferred to the USS *Hamner* (DD-718) in October 1953. On board the *Hamner*, Ken served as an electronic technician until he left the ship in early 1956 to work in the private sector and complete his four years in the inactive Navy Reserves.

Ken would later spend over thirty years collecting information about the *Hamner* and her role in the US Navy and writing her story. For those who have little knowledge of day-to-day naval operations on board a destroyer, this book is a must read.